LEARN TENSORFLOW

From Fundamentals to Practical Applications

Diego Rodrigues

LEARN TENSORFLOW

From Fundamentals to Practical Applications

2024 Edition

Author: Diego Rodrigues

Important Note

The codes and scripts presented in this book aim to illustrate the concepts discussed in the chapters, serving as practical examples. These examples were developed in custom, controlled environments, and therefore there is no guarantee that they will work fully in all scenarios. It is essential to check the configurations and customizations of the environment where they will be applied to ensure their proper functioning. We thank you for your understanding.

CONTENTS

GREETINGS!

Hello, dear reader!

It's a great honor to welcome you here, ready to dive into the world of artificial intelligence with TensorFlow. Your choice to explore this powerful tool demonstrates your vision and determination to excel in one of the most transformative areas of technology. In this book, **"Learn TensorFlow: From Fundamentals to Practical Applications - 2024 Edition"**, you'll find a comprehensive, dynamic guide designed to empower beginners and seasoned professionals alike.

Investing in your development in this era of advanced computing is a strategic decision. Deep learning and TensorFlow in particular offer immense possibilities for those who master its application. This book has been carefully crafted to be a resource for quick learning and practical application, providing the tools necessary to transform ideas into real, scalable solutions.

You are about to embark on a journey that will take you from the fundamental concepts to the most advanced techniques of artificial intelligence. Each chapter is structured to challenge your mind, encourage experimentation, and offer practical insight into how TensorFlow is shaping the future of technology. From convolutional neural networks to transferred learning and IoT applications, this book is designed to broaden your horizons and strengthen your technical skills.

Technological evolution requires professionals prepared to face complex challenges. This book is an essential resource to help you stay ahead, with in-depth insights, case studies, and practical examples that make it easy to implement robust, innovative solutions. On every page, you'll find the inspiration and knowledge you need to lead projects and create a meaningful impact in your career and society.

Prepare yourself for an enriching and challenging learning experience. Together, we'll explore the limitless potential of TensorFlow, and you'll discover how its practical application can transform the way we develop technology solutions. It's a journey of growth, discovery and excellence, and we're ready to take the first step.

Happy reading and much success!

ABOUT THE AUTHOR

www.linkedin.com/in/diegoexpertai

Best-Selling Author, Diego Rodrigues is an International Consultant and Writer specializing in Market Intelligence, Technology and Innovation. With 42 international certifications from institutions such as IBM, Google, Microsoft, AWS, Cisco, and Boston University, Ec-Council, Palo Alto and META.

Rodrigues is an expert in Artificial Intelligence, Machine Learning, Data Science, Big Data, Blockchain, Connectivity Technologies, Ethical Hacking and Threat Intelligence.

Since 2003, Rodrigues has developed more than 200 projects for important brands in Brazil, USA and Mexico. In 2024, he consolidates himself as one of the largest new generation authors of technical books in the world, with more than 180 titles published in six languages.

PREFACE/PRESENTATION OF THE BOOK

Welcome to **"LEARN TENSORFLOW: From Fundamentals to Practical Applications"**, a complete guide that will take you into the fascinating universe of deep learning. This book was carefully designed to be the bridge between initial curiosity and mastery of one of today's most powerful and versatile tools, TensorFlow.

The Artificial Intelligence (AI) revolution is reshaping the world at an impressive pace. From personalizing recommendations on streaming platforms to advances in medical diagnostics, deep learning plays a central role in many innovations. In this context, mastering a library like TensorFlow is not only a competitive differentiator, but also an opportunity to actively participate in this global transformation.

Why is this book essential for you?

With the exponential growth of deep learning applications, the demand for qualified professionals has never been higher. However, learning how to create and implement efficient models can seem like an intimidating challenge for beginners and even experienced developers. This book was designed to solve this gap, presenting TensorFlow in a practical, didactic and accessible way.

You will be guided step by step from the essential fundamentals to the most advanced applications. This guide is more than a theoretical introduction: it offers tools, examples, and insights that you can immediately apply to real projects. Our goal is to make learning TensorFlow an enriching and thought-provoking experience.

What will you find in this book?

This book is structured into 25 carefully organized chapters so that the reader can gradually evolve on their learning journey. Below, we present an overview of what each chapter will cover, highlighting their importance:

- **Chapter 1: Introduction to TensorFlow**
  Discover the history, principles, and benefits of TensorFlow. Understand why it is the preferred choice of leading companies and research institutions.
- **Chapter 2: Environment Configuration**
  Get ready to get started: learn how to install TensorFlow on different operating systems and set up your development environment efficiently.
- **Chapter 3: Tensor Fundamentals**
  Explore the fundamental building blocks of deep learning. Manipulate and transform tensors to handle data optimally.
- **Chapter 4: Data Structures in TensorFlow**
  Dive into the differences between Tensors and NumPy Arrays. Learn how to integrate data and create pipelines compatible with TensorFlow.
- **Chapter 5: Introduction to Keras**
  Discover how Keras, integrated with TensorFlow, simplifies building complex models. Discover the sequential and functional models.
- **Chapter 6: Model Training**
  Learn the training cycle, from forward pass to weight optimization, to create efficient and accurate models.
- **Chapter 7: Activation Functions**

Learn the impact of activation functions like ReLU, Sigmoid, and Softmax. Choose the most appropriate one for each problem.

- **Chapter 8: Model Regularization**
  Implement strategies like Dropout and L1/L2 penalties to avoid overfitting and create more robust models.
- **Chapter 9: Datasets and Pipelines with tf.data**
  Structure and optimize your datasets with the module tf.data. Explore advanced augmentation and batch processing techniques.
- **Chapter 10: Convolutional Networks (CNNs)**
  Discover how CNNs have revolutionized computer vision. Create powerful classifiers with TensorFlow.
- **Chapter 11: Recurrent Networks (RNNs)**
  Understand how RNNs, LSTMs and GRUs process temporal sequences and textual data. Apply them to time series and natural language processing.
- **Chapter 12: Transfer Learning**
  Save time and resources by using pre-trained models. Customize them to solve specific problems with high efficiency.
- **Chapter 13: Generative Adversarial Networks (GANs)**
  Dive into the fascinating world of GANs and learn how to create realistic image generators using TensorFlow.
- **Chapter 14: Transformers**
  Explore the fundamentals of Transformers, the architecture behind NLP models like BERT and GPT. Develop advanced language processing applications.
- **Chapter 15: Visualization with TensorBoard**
  Monitor metrics, analyze performance graphs and optimize your models with the help of TensorBoard.
- **Chapter 16: Applications in IoT**
  Discover how TensorFlow Lite lets you bring deep learning models to embedded devices and IoT solutions.
- **Chapter 17: Distributed Training**
  Accelerate large-scale model training using GPUs and

distributed clusters.

- **Chapter 18: Model Export and Deployment**
  Learn how to export and deploy models to production using tools like TensorFlow Serving and cloud services.
- **Chapter 19: Optimizers and Loss Functions**
  Master key optimizers and loss functions essential for refining model performance.
- **Chapter 20: Benchmarking and Optimization**
  Identify performance bottlenecks and implement strategies to optimize computational efficiency.
- **Chapter 21: Security and Robustness in Models**
  Create resilient models, preventing adversarial attacks and ensuring high reliability.
- **Chapter 22: Case Studies**
  Apply what you learn to real-world problems, from image classification to language models.
- **Chapter 23: TensorFlow and the Future of AI**
  Explore emerging trends and future technology directions in the field of deep learning.
- **Chapter 24: Large-Scale Applications**
  Learn how to integrate TensorFlow into enterprise systems and large projects.
- **Chapter 25: Practical Projects**
  Complete your journey with challenging and thought-provoking projects, consolidating your knowledge.

Why continue on this journey?

This book is not just a technical guide. It is an invitation for you to transform ideas into real solutions. Whether you're a curious beginner or a professional looking for new skills, mastering TensorFlow can open doors to a multitude of opportunities. As you follow the chapters, you'll discover how to apply deep learning to solve problems, innovate, and create impact in the world.

We invite you to embark on this journey with us. By the end, you will not just be a TensorFlow user, but an expert capable of leading projects that transform the future.

Happy reading and success on your learning journey!

CHAPTER 1: INTRODUCTION TO TENSORFLOW

TensorFlow is a deep learning library that has established itself as one of the most powerful and widely used tools in artificial intelligence. Created by Google in 2015, it was designed to meet the growing demand for flexible and efficient tools for developing machine learning and deep learning models. Its influence spans a wide range of industries, from healthcare and finance to transportation and technology, making it an essential choice for developers, researchers, and enterprises.

TensorFlow was born out of the need to solve complex machine learning problems in a scalable and modular way. Before TensorFlow, libraries like Theano and Torch already supported neural networks, but their adoption was limited by less intuitive interfaces and restricted support for large-scale implementations. Google developed TensorFlow to unify research and production efforts, creating a platform that offers both flexibility for experimentation and robustness for industrial deployments.

The story of TensorFlow begins with its first version, designed to replace DistBelief, Google's internal infrastructure for machine learning. By adopting a computational graphics-based paradigm, TensorFlow allowed developers to define mathematical operations as a dependency graph, facilitating execution on heterogeneous devices such as CPUs, GPUs, and TPUs. Since then, TensorFlow has evolved significantly, with the introduction of improvements such as dynamic execution with Eager Execution, greater integration with Keras, and improved support for mobile and IoT devices.

TensorFlow's impact is evident across multiple industries. In healthcare, it is used for medical image-based diagnoses, such as detecting cancer in mammograms. In the financial sector, it helps predict market trends and identify fraud. In transportation, it powers autonomous driving and route optimization systems. Its ability to process large volumes of data and train complex neural networks makes it indispensable for applications that demand high precision and performance.

One of the main features of TensorFlow is its versatility. It supports everything from small research projects to large-scale implementations in distributed clusters. Its modularity allows developers to choose between high-level APIs like Keras for a more streamlined approach or low-level APIs for full control over mathematical operations and models.

When comparing it to other deep learning libraries, some key differences emerge. PyTorch, for example, is known for its dynamic execution, which makes it easier to debug and build iterative models. TensorFlow responded to this with the introduction of Eager Execution, allowing operations to be evaluated immediately without needing to compile a static graph. While TensorFlow is widely adopted in production environments due to its stability and support tools, PyTorch is often preferred by researchers due to its less steep learning curve and syntax closer to pure Python.

Other libraries, like MXNet and Caffe, have their own niches. MXNet is popular in mobile and IoT devices due to its efficiency, while Caffe is often used in computer vision. However, TensorFlow stands out for the breadth of its ecosystem, which includes specialized libraries such as TensorFlow Lite for mobile devices, TensorFlow.js for in-browser execution, and TensorFlow Extended (TFX) for machine learning pipelines.

To understand TensorFlow's role in deep learning, it's important to explore some of its fundamental concepts. Deep learning is based on artificial neural networks, which are made up of layers of connected artificial neurons. Each layer performs mathematical operations, such as matrix multiplication and bias addition, to transform input data into predictions or internal representations. TensorFlow provides tools to create these operations in an efficient and scalable way.

A central feature of TensorFlow is its ability to train models using backpropagation, an algorithm that adjusts the weights of neural connections based on observed error. TensorFlow automates this process through its automatic differentiation engine, which calculates gradients to update weights. This allows developers to focus on the model architecture and data rather than worrying about the underlying mathematics.

For example, building a simple linear regression model can be accomplished with just a few lines of code:

python

```
import tensorflow as tf

# Defining input and output data
X = tf.constant([[1.0], [2.0], [3.0], [4.0]])
y = tf.constant([[2.0], [4.0], [6.0], [8.0]])

# Creating the model
model = tf.keras.Sequential([
    tf.keras.layers.Dense(units=1, input_shape=[1])
])

# Compiling the model
model.compile(optimizer='sgd', loss='mean_squared_error')

# Training the model
model.fit(X, y, epochs=100)
```

In this example, the model learns to adjust weights to predict and based on X using a single dense layer. The simplicity of the Keras API, integrated with TensorFlow, allows models to be built and trained quickly, while TensorFlow handles the technical details behind the scenes.

Another strength of TensorFlow is its ability to scale to distributed applications. It supports training on multiple GPUs and even clusters of machines, which is essential for dealing with large datasets and complex models. The module tf.distribute facilitates parallelization of training without requiring significant changes to existing code.

To illustrate distributed execution, consider a model trained on multiple GPUs:

python

```
import tensorflow as tf

# Distribution strategy
strategy = tf.distribute.MirroredStrategy()

# Model configuration within the strategy
with strategy.scope():
    model = tf.keras.Sequential([
        tf.keras.layers.Dense(units=128, activation='relu',
input_shape=[10]),
        tf.keras.layers.Dense(units=64, activation='relu'),
        tf.keras.layers.Dense(units=1)
    ])
    model.compile(optimizer='adam',
loss='mean_squared_error')

# Dummy data
import numpy as np
X_train = np.random.random((1000, 10))
y_train = np.random.random((1000, 1))

# Distributed training
model.fit(X_train, y_train, epochs=50, batch_size=32)
```

The ease of using distribution strategies makes TensorFlow a robust choice for industrial scenarios where efficiency is critical.

In addition to its core features, TensorFlow also supports

visualizing training metrics with TensorBoard. This tool allows you to monitor training progress, inspect gradients, and analyze model performance in real time. Integrating TensorBoard with TensorFlow is straightforward and highly beneficial for tuning models and diagnosing issues.

TensorFlow's impact goes beyond academia and industry. Its active community and extensive resources like in-depth documentation, tutorials, and hands-on examples make learning accessible for developers at all experience levels. The library also promotes continuous innovation, with frequent updates that introduce new features and enhancements.

TensorFlow's ability to span from supervised to unsupervised learning, from convolutional neural networks to Transformer-based models, and from mobile devices to cloud clusters highlights its versatility. Mastering TensorFlow means not only acquiring a technical skill, but also opening doors to contribute to one of the most dynamic and transformative fields in technology.

CHAPTER 2: ENVIRONMENT CONFIGURATION

Setting up a suitable development environment is the first step to ensuring efficiency and productivity when working with TensorFlow. Choosing and configuring your environment correctly ensures projects run smoothly, optimizing performance and avoiding compatibility errors. Detailed below are the steps for installing and configuring TensorFlow on popular operating systems, as well as creating virtual environments for organized projects.

Installation on Windows

On the Windows operating system, installing TensorFlow requires attention to compatibility details. TensorFlow can be installed using pip, the Python package manager. It is essential to ensure that prerequisites, such as the correct Python version and required libraries, are installed.

First, make sure Python is installed. Access the terminal or command prompt and run:

bash

```
python --version
```

If Python is not installed, download it from the official website (https://www.python.org) and install the recommended version (3.8 or higher). Make sure to select the "Add Python to PATH" option during installation.

After verifying or installing Python, update the package manager pip:

bash

```
python -m pip install --upgrade pip
```

With the pip updated, install TensorFlow using the command:

bash

```
pip install tensorflow
```

For machines with NVIDIA GPUs, CUDA support can be enabled to speed up calculations. Install the latest NVIDIA drivers, CUDA toolkit and cuDNN available on the official NVIDIA website. After installation, check if TensorFlow recognizes the GPU:

python

```
import tensorflow as tf
print("GPU disponível:", tf.config.list_physical_devices('GPU'))
```

This command returns a list of available GPUs. If no GPU is detected, review the CUDA and cuDNN settings.

Installation on macOS

On macOS, TensorFlow can be installed directly using pip. Go to the terminal and update Python and pip:

bash

```
brew install python
python3 -m pip install --upgrade pip
```

Install TensorFlow with:

bash

```
pip install tensorflow-macos
```

While TensorFlow supports the Metal deep learning accelerator on macOS, which improves performance on Apple GPUs, it does not support CUDA as Apple devices do not use NVIDIA GPUs.

After installation, test that TensorFlow is configured correctly:

python

```
import tensorflow as tf
print(tf.reduce_sum(tf.random.normal([1000, 1000])))
```

If the operation runs without errors, TensorFlow is ready to use.

Installation on Linux

Linux is widely used in machine learning due to its stability and flexibility. To install TensorFlow, ensure that core dependencies such as Python and pip, are installed.

Update system repositories:

bash

```
sudo apt update && sudo apt upgrade
```

Install dependencies:

bash

```
sudo apt install python3 python3-pip python3-venv
```

Install TensorFlow with:

bash

```
pip install tensorflow
```

To enable GPU support, install the NVIDIA drivers, CUDA Toolkit, and cuDNN. After configuring the GPU, test its availability in TensorFlow:

python

```
import tensorflow as tf
print("GPU disponível:", tf.config.list_physical_devices('GPU'))
```

Installation on Google Colab

Google Colab is a cloud-based platform that provides free access to GPUs and TPUs. It is an excellent option for those who do not have locally advanced hardware.

Access Google Colab at https://colab.research.google.com and create a new notebook. By default, TensorFlow is already installed. To check the installed version:

python

```
import tensorflow as tf
print("TensorFlow version:", tf.__version__)
```

If you need a specific version, install it directly on your notebook:

bash

```
!pip install tensorflow==2.12.0
```

Enable GPU usage by going to **Runtime > Change runtime type** and selecting "GPU". After that, run:

python

```
import tensorflow as tf
print("Available device:", tf.test.gpu_device_name())
```

This configuration makes Colab an ideal tool for experimentation and model training without the need to invest in hardware.

Creation of Virtual Environments

The creation of virtual environments is essential to maintain isolated projects and avoid dependency conflicts between different projects. Python offers built-in tools for creating and managing virtual environments, such as venv.

To create a virtual environment, choose the directory where you want to store it and run:

bash

```
python -m venv my_env
```

Replace my_env by the name of the environment. Activate the virtual environment with:

No Windows:

bash

```
my_env\Scripts\activate
```

No macOS/Linux:

bash

```
source my_env/bin/activate
```

When the virtual environment is activated, the prompt will indicate the name of the environment. Within this environment, install TensorFlow:

bash

```
pip install tensorflow
```

To disable the virtual environment, use:

bash

```
deactivate
```

This process ensures that each project uses specific versions of libraries, avoiding conflicts.

Additional Configuration with Docker

Docker is a powerful alternative for setting up machine learning environments. It creates isolated containers that include all necessary dependencies.

Install Docker and download the official TensorFlow image:

bash

```
docker pull tensorflow/tensorflow:latest
```

To launch an interactive container:

bash

```
docker run -it --rm tensorflow/tensorflow:latest bash
```

In the container, TensorFlow is already pre-installed. To use GPUs, make sure Docker supports the NVIDIA Container Toolkit.

bash

```
docker run --gpus all -it tensorflow/tensorflow:latest-gpu bash
```

This method is useful for reproducing identical environments on different systems.

Testing and Validating the Installation

After configuring the environment, it is important to validate that TensorFlow was installed correctly and is working as expected. A simple test involves performing basic operations:

python

```
import tensorflow as tf
```

```
# Creating a tensor
tensor = tf.constant([[1.0, 2.0], [3.0, 4.0]])

# Matrix multiplication
result = tf.matmul(tensor, tensor)

print("Multiplication result:", result)
```

This run verifies that basic mathematical operations work without errors.

Correctly setting up the environment is a crucial step to ensuring efficiency and success when developing with TensorFlow. Whether using on-premises systems, cloud-based platforms, or containers, each method has specific advantages for different scenarios. Organizing with virtual environments and using GPUs or TPUs optimizes performance, setting the stage for the development of innovative deep learning solutions.

CHAPTER 3: TENSOR FUNDAMENTALS

Tensors are the fundamental elements in deep learning, being used to represent and manipulate data efficiently. In TensorFlow, tensors are multidimensional structures that can contain data such as integers, floating-point numbers, Booleans, or other types. They are generalizations of matrices and vectors that support advanced mathematical operations on accelerated hardware such as GPUs and TPUs. Mastering the concepts and operations with tensors is essential to working with deep learning and machine learning effectively.

Tensors can be created in different ways in TensorFlow, including from arrays, lists, or other data structures. Each tensor has properties such as shape, data type (dtype) and device where it is located. The flexibility of tensors allows them to represent simple data, such as scalar numbers, to complex structures, such as images, videos or time series.

Tensor creation can be accomplished with dedicated TensorFlow functions. To create a constant tensor, use the function `tf.constant`:

python

```
import tensorflow as tf

# Creating a constant tensor
tensor_constant = tf.constant([[1, 2], [3, 4]])

print("Constant tensor:")
print(tensor_constant)
```

The created tensor has two axes (dimensions) and stores the given values as a nested list. The property shape allows you to check the dimensions of the tensioner:

python

```
print("Forma do tensor:", tensor_constant.shape)
```

Tensor manipulation is a central part of deep learning. Operations like addition, multiplication, and other transformations are applied to prepare data before training it in deep learning models. Tensor multiplication can be performed with the function tf.matmul for matrix multiplication or with the operator * for element-by-element operations:

python

```
# Matrix multiplication
tensor_a = tf.constant([[1, 2], [3, 4]])
tensor_b = tf.constant([[5, 6], [7, 8]])

matrix_multiplication = tf.matmul(tensor_a, tensor_b)
print("Matrix multiplication:")
print(matrix_multiplication)

# Element-to-element multiplication
element_wise_multiplication = tensor_a * tensor_b
print("Element-by-element multiplication:")
print(element_wise_multiplication)
```

The differences between these operations reflect the use of tensors in varying contexts, such as processing numerical data or images.

Tensors also support indexing and slicing to access subsets of data. This functionality is crucial when dealing with large volumes of information organized in batches. To access a specific row or element:

python

```
# Selecting a line
row = tensor_constant[0]
print("First line:")
print(row)

# Selecting an element
element = tensor_constant[0, 1]
print("Element at position [0, 1]:", element)
```

Tensors can be resized to meet model input needs. The function tf.reshape is used to change the shape of a tensor without modifying the underlying data:

python

```
# Resizing the tensor
reshaped_tensor = tf.reshape(tensor_constant, [4, 1])
print("Resized Tensor:")
print(reshaped_tensor)
```

Flexibility in resizing is especially useful in tasks such as image processing, where data often needs to be adapted to different layers of the neural network.

In addition to basic operations, tensors can be manipulated in advanced ways to perform complex operations. Reduction operations such as sum and average are often used to calculate metrics or fit data:

python

```
# Sum of elements
sum_elements = tf.reduce_sum(tensor_constant)
print("Sum of all elements:", sum_elements)

# Average of elements
mean_elements = tf.reduce_mean(tensor_constant)
print("Mean of elements:", mean_elements)
```

Such operations make tensors extremely versatile for

representing and processing data in deep learning.

TensorFlow also supports transpose and inversion operations, which are useful in many deep learning algorithms:

python

```
# Tensor transposition
transposed_tensor = tf.transpose(tensor_constant)
print("Transposed Tensor:")
print(transposed_tensor)

# Creating a tensor for inversion
tensor_for_inversion = tf.constant([[1.0, 2.0], [3.0, 4.0]])
inverted_tensor = tf.linalg.inv(tensor_for_inversion)
print("Inverted Tensor:")
print(inverted_tensor)
```

Transposition rearranges the tensor axes, while inversion is applied to square floating-point tensors.

Using tensors on GPUs or TPUs significantly speeds up operations. To transfer a tensor to the GPU, use:

python

```
# Transferring the tensor to the GPU
tensor_on_gpu = tensor_constant.gpu()
print("Tensor allocated on GPU:", tensor_on_gpu)
```

TensorFlow automatically manages the allocation of tensors across available devices, ensuring efficiency in training and inference.

Tensors are especially powerful in deep learning because of their support for automatic gradient calculation. Configuring a tensor with the property `requires_grad` allows you to automatically calculate gradients to optimize models. Calculating gradients is essential in the backpropagation process, where the neural network weights are adjusted to minimize the loss function.

python

```
# Creating a tensor with gradients enabled
x = tf.Variable(3.0)

# Defining a function
with tf.GradientTape() as tape:
    y = x**2

# Calculating the gradient
gradient = tape.gradient(y, x)
print("Gradient:", gradient)
```

TensorFlow's flexibility in automatically calculating gradients eliminates the need to implement differentiation manually, simplifying the development of complex models.

Tensors can also be combined to create larger structures, such as images or time series. Concatenation operations allow you to join data along a specific axis:

python

```
# Concatenating tensors
tensor_c = tf.constant([[1, 2]])
tensor_d = tf.constant([[3, 4]])
concatenated_tensor = tf.concat([tensor_c, tensor_d], axis=0)
print("Tensor concatenado:")
print(concatenated_tensor)
```

Concatenation is widely used for data preprocessing and batching during training.

Another important transformation is broadcast, which allows you to perform operations between tensors of different shapes, automatically adjusting the smaller dimensions:

python

```
# Broadcast between tensors
tensor_small = tf.constant([1, 2, 3])
tensor_large = tf.constant([[1], [2], [3]])
```

```
broadcast_result = tensor_small + tensor_large
print("Broadcast result:")
print(broadcast_result)
```

Broadcast simplifies operations between tensors without the need for manual resizing, increasing code efficiency and clarity.

Tensors form the basis of all calculations in deep learning and machine learning, allowing you to manipulate data in an efficient and scalable way. Understanding basic and advanced tensor operations is essential for developing models that deal with complex data, providing insights and innovative solutions in several areas.

CHAPTER 4: DATA STRUCTURES IN TENSORFLOW

Data structures in TensorFlow are designed to provide efficiency and flexibility in deep learning. Tensors, being the basic unit of data in TensorFlow, are optimized for mathematical operations and computation on accelerated hardware such as GPUs and TPUs. When working with TensorFlow, it is essential to understand the differences between tensors and NumPy arrays, as well as ways to manipulate datasets and integrate them with external APIs.

Differences between Tensors and NumPy Arrays

TensorFlow tensors and NumPy arrays share many similarities, such as being multidimensional structures for storing data and performing elementary mathematical operations. However, there are fundamental differences that make them suitable for different scenarios.

1. **Immutability and Flexibility**
   Tensors are immutable, which means that once created, their values cannot be changed. This characteristic makes them safe to use in parallel operations, common in deep learning. NumPy arrays, on the other hand, are mutable, allowing their values to be changed after creation.
2. **Accelerated Computing Support**
   Tensors can run on CPUs, GPUs, or TPUs, while NumPy

arrays are limited to CPUs. The ability to allocate tensors directly to accelerated devices is one of the biggest benefits of TensorFlow.

3. **Integration with Gradients**
   Tensors in TensorFlow have built-in support for automatic gradient calculation, used in model training. NumPy arrays do not natively support this functionality.
4. **Efficiency and Scalability**
   TensorFlow is optimized for large-scale operations, handling batches of data efficiently. NumPy is best suited for smaller tasks or operations that do not require parallelism or distributed execution.

Creating a tensor and a NumPy array demonstrates the similarities and differences between the two:

python

```
import tensorflow as tf
import numpy as np

# Creating a tensor
tensor = tf.constant([[1.0, 2.0], [3.0, 4.0]])
print("Tensor:")
print(tensor)

# Creating a NumPy array
array = np.array([[1.0, 2.0], [3.0, 4.0]])
print("Array NumPy:")
print(array)
```

Basic operations, such as addition and multiplication, can be performed on both tensors and arrays. However, TensorFlow allows you to perform these operations on GPUs or TPUs:

python

```
# Sum of tensors
tensor_sum = tf.add(tensor, tensor)
```

```
print("Soma of tensors:")
print(tensor_sum)

# Soma de arrays NumPy
array_sum = np.add(array, array)
print("Soma de arrays NumPy:")
print(array_sum)
```

To convert between tensors and arrays, TensorFlow provides convenient functions:

python

```
# Converting tensor to NumPy array
tensor_to_array = tensor.numpy()
print("Tensor para Array NumPy:")
print(tensor_to_array)

# Converting NumPy array to tensor
array_to_tensor = tf.convert_to_tensor(array)
print("Array NumPy para Tensor:")
print(array_to_tensor)
```

Interoperability between tensors and arrays is useful for integrating TensorFlow with NumPy-based scientific libraries.

Dataset Manipulation

Dataset manipulation is a critical component in deep learning. The module tf.data TensorFlow offers tools to efficiently create and manipulate datasets, allowing you to load, transform, and organize data for model training and evaluation.

Datasets in TensorFlow are represented as objects tf.data.Dataset. A dataset can be created from arrays, files or other data sources. To create a dataset from lists or arrays:

python

```
# Creating a dataset from lists
```

```
data = [1, 2, 3, 4, 5]
dataset = tf.data.Dataset.from_tensor_slices(data)
print("Dataset created from lists:")
for element in dataset:
    print(element.numpy())
```

Reading CSV files or other formats is made easier with tf.data.experimental.make_csv_dataset, which converts files into datasets ready for training:

python

```
# Creating a dataset from a CSV file
csv_file = "data.csv" # Replace with CSV file path
csv_dataset = tf.data.experimental.make_csv_dataset(
    csv_file,
    batch_size=2,
    num_epochs=1
)

print("Dataset created from CSV:")
for batch in csv_dataset:
    print(batch)
```

Datasets can be transformed with operations such as mapping, filtering and batch grouping. The function map allows you to apply transformations to each element of the dataset:

python

```
# Applying transformation to each element
transformed_dataset = dataset.map(lambda x: x * 2)
print("Transformed dataset:")
for element in transformed_dataset:
    print(element.numpy())
```

Data batching and shuffling are essential for efficient training:

python

```
# Splitting the dataset into batches
```

```
batched_dataset = dataset.batch(2)
print("Batch dataset:")
for batch in batched_dataset:
    print(batch.numpy())

# Shuffling the dataset
shuffled_dataset = dataset.shuffle(buffer_size=5)
print("Shuffled dataset:")
for element in shuffled_dataset:
    print(element.numpy())
```

THE tf.data It is highly scalable and can be used to process large volumes of data, including images and text.

Integration with External APIs

TensorFlow allows integration with external APIs to load and process complex data such as images, videos or text. The module tf.keras.preprocessing provides tools for handling images and text. For images, the function image_dataset_from_directory load images from a directory:

python

```
# Loading images from a directory
image_dataset = tf.keras.utils.image_dataset_from_directory(
    "path_to_images",
    batch_size=32,
    image_size=(224, 224)
)
print("Image dataset:")
for images, labels in image_dataset.take(1):
    print(images.shape)
    print(labels)
```

The generated dataset can be pre-processed with transformations such as normalization or augmentation:

python

```
# Normalizing images
normalized_dataset = image_dataset.map(lambda x, y: (x /
255.0, y))
print("Normalized image dataset:")
for images, labels in normalized_dataset.take(1):
    print(images[0])
```

For text, TensorFlow supports text tokenizer Tokenizer to transform text into sequences of numbers:

python

```
# Tokenizing text
texts = ["TensorFlow is powerful", "Learning TensorFlow is
essential"]
tokenizer = tf.keras.preprocessing.text.Tokenizer()
tokenizer.fit_on_texts(texts)
sequences = tokenizer.texts_to_sequences(texts)
print("Tokenized text:")
print(sequences)
```

Manipulating data using external APIs allows you to integrate TensorFlow with complex, customizable data pipelines.

Mastering data structures in TensorFlow and integration with external APIs are fundamental to creating robust and efficient pipelines, from data ingestion to transformation and loading for training. These tools optimize your workflow and allow you to work with different types of data at scale.

CHAPTER 5: INTRODUCTION TO KERAS

The Keras API is a high-level interface that simplifies the creation, training, and evaluation of deep learning models. Fully integrated with TensorFlow, it combines ease of use with performance, allowing developers to implement complex neural networks intuitively and efficiently. Designed to be modular and extensible, Keras provides abstractions that make deep learning accessible to beginners and seasoned professionals alike.

Keras API Overview

Keras was created with the goal of accelerating neural network prototyping without sacrificing control over model details. This philosophy is implemented through several advantages:

1. **Easy to use**
   Keras uses a clear and concise syntax, making model development faster and more readable.
2. **Modularity**
   Core components such as layers, optimizers, and loss functions can be flexibly combined to create custom models.
3. **Integration with TensorFlow**
   Since its integration with TensorFlow, Keras benefits from the library's entire infrastructure, including running on accelerated hardware and tools like TensorBoard.

4. **Support for multiple paradigms**
   Keras supports two main model building styles: sequential, ideal for simple architectures, and functional, which allows you to create complex models with branches or multiple inputs and outputs.

Creating a sequential model

The sequential model is the simplest way to build a neural network with Keras. It organizes the layers in a linear manner, where the output of one layer is used as the input of the next. This approach is suitable for feedforward neural networks, which are widely used in classification and regression.

To create a sequential model, import the API Sequential and add layers using the class Dense:

python

```
import tensorflow as tf
from tensorflow.keras import Sequential
from tensorflow.keras.layers import Dense

# Creating a sequential model
model = Sequential([
    Dense(units=64, activation='relu', input_shape=(10,)),
    Dense(units=32, activation='relu'),
    Dense(units=1, activation='sigmoid')
])

# Model summary
model.summary()
```

The first layer specifies the number of units (neurons), the activation function (resume) and the input dimension. Subsequent layers automatically inherit the format of the previous output.

Compiling and training a sequential model

Before training, the model needs to be compiled. The compilation defines the optimizer, loss function, and evaluation metrics:

python

```
# Compiling the model
model.compile(
    optimizer='adam',
    loss='binary_crossentropy',
    metrics=['accuracy']
)
```

The optimizer adam It is widely used due to its efficiency in adjusting weights. The loss function binary_crossentropy is suitable for binary classification problems.

To train the model, use the function fit, providing the input data, the corresponding labels and the number of epochs:

python

```
# Dummy data
import numpy as np
X_train = np.random.random((1000, 10))
y_train = np.random.randint(0, 2, size=(1000,))

# Training the model
model.fit(X_train, y_train, epochs=10, batch_size=32)
```

After training, the model can be evaluated with the function evaluate and used to make predictions with predict:

python

```
# Model evaluation
X_test = np.random.random((200, 10))
y_test = np.random.randint(0, 2, size=(200,))
loss, accuracy = model.evaluate(X_test, y_test)
```

```
print(f"Loss: {loss}, Accuracy: {accuracy}")

# Making predictions
predictions = model.predict(X_test[:5])
print("Forecasts:")
print(predictions)
```

Creating a working model

Keras' functional API offers greater flexibility, enabling the creation of complex architectures. Instead of building the model as a linear sequence of layers, each layer is treated as an independent object, allowing for custom connections.

To create a working model, start with an input tensor and chain operations to define the connections between layers:

python

```
from tensorflow.keras import Model
from tensorflow.keras.layers import Input, Dense

# Defining the input tensor
inputs = Input(shape=(10,))

# Connecting layers
x = Dense(64, activation='relu')(inputs)
x = Dense(32, activation='relu')(x)
outputs = Dense(1, activation='sigmoid')(x)

# Creating the functional model
model = Model(inputs=inputs, outputs=outputs)

# Model summary
model.summary()
```

This style is ideal for architectures that require forks, multiple inputs or outputs. An example of a model with multiple outputs:

python

```
# Model with multiple outputs
x1 = Dense(64, activation='relu')(inputs)
x2 = Dense(32, activation='relu')(x1)
output1 = Dense(1, activation='sigmoid')(x1)
output2 = Dense(1, activation='linear')(x2)

model = Model(inputs=inputs, outputs=[output1, output2])
model.summary()
```

To train models with multiple outputs, use a dictionary to specify loss functions and weights:

python

```
# Compilation of the model with multiple outputs
model.compile(
    optimizer='adam',
    loss={'dense_1': 'binary_crossentropy', 'dense_2': 'mse'},
    loss_weights={'dense_1': 0.5, 'dense_2': 0.5}
)

# Training with multiple outputs
y_train_1 = np.random.randint(0, 2, size=(1000,))
y_train_2 = np.random.random(size=(1000,))
model.fit(X_train, {'dense_1': y_train_1, 'dense_2': y_train_2},
epochs=10)
```

Customization and extensibility

Keras allows you to create custom layers to meet specific requirements. Subclass the class Layer to define new operations:

python

```
from tensorflow.keras.layers import Layer

# Defining a custom layer
class CustomLayer(Layer):
    def __init__(self, units, activation=None):
        super(CustomLayer, self).__init__()
        self.units = units
        self.activation = tf.keras.activations.get(activation)

    def build(self, input_shape):
        self.kernel = self.add_weight(
            shape=(input_shape[-1], self.units),
            initializer='random_normal',
            trainable=True
        )

    def call(self, inputs):
        return self.activation(tf.matmul(inputs, self.kernel))

# Using custom layer
inputs = Input(shape=(10,))
x = CustomLayer(32, activation='relu')(inputs)
outputs = Dense(1, activation='sigmoid')(x)
model = Model(inputs=inputs, outputs=outputs)
model.summary()
```

Custom layers expand the potential for creating innovative models tailored to specific use cases.

Integration with callbacks

Keras callbacks allow you to customize training behavior, such as saving checkpoints, adjusting the learning rate, or stopping training early. Add callbacks with the parameter `callbacks` in function `fit`:

python

```
from tensorflow.keras.callbacks import EarlyStopping,
```

```
ModelCheckpoint

# Defining callbacks
early_stopping = EarlyStopping(monitor='val_loss', patience=5)
checkpoint = ModelCheckpoint('best_model.h5',
save_best_only=True)

# Training with callbacks
model.fit(
    X_train,
    y_train,
    epochs=50,
    batch_size=32,
    validation_split=0.2,
    callbacks=[early_stopping, checkpoint]
)
```

Callbacks optimize the training process and help prevent overfitting.

Keras and simplicity in deep learning

The Keras API, with its intuitive and powerful approach, makes deep learning accessible to everyone. Its sequential and functional models cover a wide range of use cases, from simple problems to advanced architectures. The ability to customize and integrate with TensorFlow ensures that developers can create robust and scalable solutions, adapting to the demands of real projects.

CHAPTER 6: MODEL TRAINING

Training deep learning models is a structured process that involves three main steps: the forward pass, error calculation, and updating the weights. This iterative cycle is known as backpropagation and is the foundation for tuning model parameters to achieve the best performance. To maximize training efficiency, it is critical to understand underlying concepts such as hyperparameter configuration and the role of loss functions and optimizers.

Forward Pass and Error Calculation

The forward pass is the initial step in training a model. At this stage, the input data passes through the layers of the neural network, generating a predicted output. During this operation, each layer performs mathematical transformations on the data based on current weights and activation functions.

A simple binary classification model demonstrates how forward pass occurs:

python

```
import tensorflow as tf
from tensorflow.keras import Sequential
from tensorflow.keras.layers import Dense

# Defining the model
model = Sequential([
    Dense(units=16, activation='relu', input_shape=(8,)),
    Dense(units=8, activation='relu'),
    Dense(units=1, activation='sigmoid')
```

```
])

# Model summary
model.summary()

# Dummy data
X = tf.random.normal((5, 8))

# Forward pass: generating predictions
predictions = model(X)
print("Predictions:")
print(predictions)
```

After the forward pass, the model calculates the error by comparing the predicted output with the actual values. This error, or loss, is a fundamental metric that directs the adjustment of the network's weights.

python

```
# Actual values
y_true = tf.constant([[0], [1], [0], [1], [0]], dtype=tf.float32)

# Binary loss function
loss_fn = tf.keras.losses.BinaryCrossentropy()
loss = loss_fn(y_true, predictions)
print("Calculated loss:", loss.numpy())
```

Backpropagation and Weight Update

Backpropagation uses the calculated error to adjust the weights of the neural network. This step is based on the derivative chain rule, allowing the error to propagate from the end of the network to previous layers. During backpropagation, TensorFlow automatically calculates the gradients of the weights with respect to the loss function.

python

```
# Creating a gradient ribbon
with tf.GradientTape() as tape:
```

```
    predictions = model(X)
    loss = loss_fn(y_true, predictions)

# Calculating gradients
gradients = tape.gradient(loss, model.trainable_variables)
print("Gradients:")
for grad in gradients:
    print(grad.numpy())
```

The calculated gradients are used to update the neural network weights. The optimizer, like Adam, applies these updates efficiently, adjusting weights to reduce loss.

python

```
# Defining the optimizer
optimizer = tf.keras.optimizers.Adam()

# Applying gradients
optimizer.apply_gradients(zip(gradients,
model.trainable_variables))
```

This combination of calculating gradients and applying updates constitutes the basic training cycle.

Configuring Hyperparameters for Better Performance

Hyperparameters control the model's behavior during training and have a significant impact on learning efficiency and accuracy. Tuning these parameters is essential to achieving optimal performance.

1. **Learning Rate**
   The learning rate defines the size of the steps taken by the optimizer when adjusting the weights. Too high rates can cause instability, while too low rates can result in slow training.

python

```
# Configuring an optimizer with custom learning rate
optimizer = tf.keras.optimizers.Adam(learning_rate=0.001)
```

2. **Lot Size**
   The batch size determines how many data samples are processed before the weights are updated. Smaller sizes can speed up initial training, but larger sizes tend to converge to more stable solutions.

python

```
# Adjusting batch size in training
model.fit(X, y_true, batch_size=16, epochs=10)
```

3. **Number of Epochs**
   The number of epochs defines how many times the model traverses the entire dataset during training. Setting an appropriate number of epochs helps avoid underfitting or overfitting.

python

```
# Training the model with custom number of epochs
model.fit(X, y_true, epochs=20)
```

4. **Regularization**
   Techniques like Dropout or L2 penalties help avoid overfitting by reducing model complexity.

python

```
from tensorflow.keras.layers import Dropout

# Adding a Dropout layer
model = Sequential([
    Dense(units=16, activation='relu', input_shape=(8,)),
```

```
    Dropout(rate=0.5),
    Dense(units=1, activation='sigmoid')
])
```

5. **Loss Function**
   Choosing the appropriate loss function is crucial. Regression problems may use mean squared errors, while binary or multiclass classification tasks require cross-entropy.

python

```
# Configuring loss functions for different tasks
loss_fn_regression = tf.keras.losses.MeanSquaredError()
loss_fn_classification =
tf.keras.losses.CategoricalCrossentropy()
```

Complete Training Cycle

Integrating all these steps results in the complete training cycle of a model. The API fit TensorFlow abstracts many of these operations, but you can customize the cycle to meet specific requirements.

python

```
# Simulated data
X_train = tf.random.normal((1000, 8))
y_train = tf.random.uniform((1000, 1), minval=0, maxval=2,
dtype=tf.int32)

# Compiling the model
model.compile(
    optimizer='adam',
    loss='binary_crossentropy',
    metrics=['accuracy']
)

# Training
```

```
history = model.fit(X_train, y_train, batch_size=32, epochs=10)

# Assessment
X_test = tf.random.normal((200, 8))
y_test = tf.random.uniform((200, 1), minval=0, maxval=2,
dtype=tf.int32)
loss, accuracy = model.evaluate(X_test, y_test)
print(f"Loss: {loss}, Accuracy: {accuracy}")
```

Training history can be used to view metrics and tune hyperparameters for continuous improvement.

Fine Tuning and Advanced Training

After initial training, techniques such as hyperparameter fine-tuning or transfer learning can be applied to improve model performance. Fine-tuning involves exploring combinations of parameters, while transfer learning uses pre-trained models to speed up training.

python

```
from tensorflow.keras.applications import MobileNetV2

# Loading a pre-trained model
base_model = MobileNetV2(input_shape=(128, 128, 3),
include_top=False, weights='imagenet')

# Freezing base model weights
base_model.trainable = False

# Adding custom layers
inputs = tf.keras.Input(shape=(128, 128, 3))
x = base_model(inputs, training=False)
x = tf.keras.layers.GlobalAveragePooling2D()(x)
outputs = tf.keras.layers.Dense(1, activation='sigmoid')(x)

model = tf.keras.Model(inputs, outputs)

# Compiling and training the model
model.compile(optimizer='adam', loss='binary_crossentropy',
```

```
metrics=['accuracy'])
model.fit(X_train, y_train, epochs=5)
```

Continuously adjusting the weights allows the model to achieve better generalization, even across specific data sets.

Training models involves deeply understanding the learning cycle and continually tuning hyperparameters to achieve optimal performance. By combining automated TensorFlow tools and advanced customizations, you can create models that address a wide range of deep learning challenges.

CHAPTER 7: ACTIVATION FUNCTIONS

Activation functions are essential components in neural networks, responsible for introducing non-linearity to models. They determine how neurons process input signals and, consequently, how networks learn complex patterns from data. This chapter explores the most used activation functions, such as ReLU, Sigmoid, Tanh and Softmax, analyzing their characteristics, practical applications and the appropriate choice for different problems.

The Role of Activation Functions

Activation functions transform the weighted sums of a neuron's inputs into an output that can be used in subsequent layers. Without these functions, neural networks would be equivalent to a simple linear combination, unable to model complex data. By introducing nonlinearity, activation functions allow networks to learn patterns such as edges in images, contexts in text, and trends in time series.

Analysis of Main Activation Functions

ReLU (Rectified Linear Unit)

ReLU is one of the most popular and widely used activation functions due to its simplicity and computational efficiency. It returns zero for negative values and the value itself for positive values.

python

```
import tensorflow as tf

# Applying ReLU to tensors
inputs = tf.constant([-2.0, -1.0, 0.0, 1.0, 2.0])
outputs = tf.nn.relu(inputs)
print(outputs.numpy())
```

Features:

- Simplicity: Easy to implement and computationally efficient.
- Sparsity effect: Many neurons remain inactive (zero output) for negative inputs, which reduces computational cost.
- Dead gradient problem: Neurons can "die" when repeatedly reset to zero gradients.

Applications:
ReLU is widely used in convolutional networks (CNNs) for tasks such as image classification and object detection, due to its consistent performance and ability to scale well with large data.

Sigmoid

The Sigmoid function is an S-shaped curve that maps input values to the range between 0 and 1. It is often used for binary classification tasks.

python

```
# Applying Sigmoid to tensors
outputs = tf.nn.sigmoid(inputs)
print(outputs.numpy())
```

Features:

- Produces smooth, bounded values useful for interpreting as probabilities.
- Propensity for gradient disappearance: For extreme input values, gradients become very small, making learning difficult.

Applications:
Sigmoid is commonly used in the output layer of networks for binary classification, such as fraud detection or sentiment analysis.

Tanh (Hyperbolic Tangent)

The Tanh function is similar to Sigmoid, but it maps values to the range between -1 and 1. This causes the outputs to be centered around zero.

python

```
# Applying Tanh to tensors
outputs = tf.nn.tanh(inputs)
print(outputs.numpy())
```

Features:

- Better centering: Compared to Sigmoid, it produces larger gradients for values close to zero, making it more efficient in initial learning.
- It also suffers from the problem of gradient disappearance

at extreme values.

Applications:
Tanh is used in tasks that require centralized outputs, such as recurrent networks (RNNs) and time series processing.

Softmax

Softmax is an activation function used for multiclass classification tasks, converting outputs into probabilities that sum to 1.

python

```
# Applying Softmax to tensors
logits = tf.constant([1.0, 2.0, 3.0])
outputs = tf.nn.softmax(logits)
print(outputs.numpy())
```

Features:

- It produces probability distributions, facilitating the interpretation of results.
- Sensitive to extreme values: Very large inputs can lead to results dominated by a single class.

Applications:
Softmax is widely used in the output layer of networks designed for multi-class classification tasks such as image categorization or text analysis.

Choosing Activation Functions for Different Problems

Choosing the appropriate activation function depends on the type of task, network architecture, and data characteristics. Below are some general guidelines for selecting the correct activation function:

1. **Convolutional Networks (CNNs)**
   ReLU is the default choice for CNNs due to its efficiency and performance in computer vision tasks.
2. **Recurrent Networks (RNNs)**
   Tanh is often used in recurrent networks such as LSTMs and GRUs to process time series and sequences.
3. **Binary Classification**
   Sigmoid is ideal for binary classification outputs as it maps values to the range [0, 1], interpretable as probability.
4. **Multiclass Classification**
   Softmax is used in multiclass classification problems to convert outputs into normalized probabilities.
5. **Deep Networks**
   More advanced functions such as Leaky ReLU and Parametric ReLU (PReLU) can be considered for very deep networks where dead gradient is a concern.

Customizing Activation Functions

In addition to the standard functions, you can create custom activation functions for specific needs. TensorFlow makes it easy to implement custom functions:

python

```
# Creating a custom activation function
def custom_activation(x):
    return tf.maximum(0.1 * x, x)  # Leaky ReLU

# Using the function in the model
from tensorflow.keras.layers import Dense
```

```
layer = Dense(128, activation=custom_activation)
```

Custom functions are useful for adapting models to specific problems, optimizing performance.

Impact of Activation Functions on Convergence

The choice of activation function directly impacts the model's convergence, that is, its ability to minimize the loss function during training. Some important considerations include:

- **Convergence Speed**: Functions like ReLU tend to speed up training due to the simplicity of their calculations.
- **Gradient Stability**: Functions like Tanh and Sigmoid can introduce instabilities in deep networks due to gradient disappearance.

Understanding activation functions and their applications is essential for designing effective neural networks. Each function has specific advantages and limitations, and the appropriate choice depends on the problem at hand. Experimenting with different activation functions in practical projects is an effective way to discover how each one behaves in real-world scenarios, improving your ability to solve complex problems with deep learning.

CHAPTER 8: MODEL REGULARIZATION

Regularization is a set of fundamental techniques in deep learning that helps reduce overfitting and improve model generalization. Overfitting occurs when the model learns specific patterns from the training set, including noise, but does not generalize well to new data. Regularization techniques, such as Dropout, L1 and L2 penalties, work by limiting the complexity of the model, encouraging it to learn more robust patterns.

Regularization Concept

Regularization works by adding constraints or modifications to the model's training so that it focuses on the essential aspects of the data and ignores irrelevant patterns. These techniques can be implemented directly in the network architecture, in loss functions, or as additional processes during training.

Dropout

Dropout is one of the most popular regularization techniques. It works by randomly deactivating a percentage of neurons during training, forcing the model not to rely on specific combinations of activations. This approach creates "smaller" networks in each iteration, promoting greater robustness.

Implementing Dropout in TensorFlow is straightforward, using the Dropout. Below is an example of a template that incorporates Dropout:

python

```
import tensorflow as tf
from tensorflow.keras import Sequential
from tensorflow.keras.layers import Dense, Dropout

# Creating the model with Dropout
model = Sequential([
    Dense(units=128, activation='relu', input_shape=(100,)),
    Dropout(rate=0.5), # 50% of neurons will be deactivated
during training
    Dense(units=64, activation='relu'),
    Dropout(rate=0.3), # 30% of neurons will be deactivated
    Dense(units=10, activation='softmax')
])

# Model summary
model.summary()
```

During training, Dropout is automatically enabled, but is disabled in the inference phase, ensuring that all activations are available.

python

```
# Compiling the model
model.compile(
    optimizer='adam',
    loss='sparse_categorical_crossentropy',
    metrics=['accuracy']
)

# Generating dummy data
import numpy as np
X_train = np.random.random((1000, 100))
y_train = np.random.randint(0, 10, size=(1000,))

# Training the model
model.fit(X_train, y_train, epochs=10, batch_size=32)
```

Dropout is highly effective in problems where overfitting is evident, such as deep networks and small datasets.

L1 and L2 Penalties

The L1 and L2 penalties add regularization terms directly to the model loss function. These terms penalize excessively large weights, reducing model complexity.

- **L1 (Lasso Regularization):** Encourages weight sparsity, i.e. sets many weights to zero. This can be useful when some inputs are irrelevant.
- **L2 (Ridge Regularization):** It penalizes large weights, but does not force them to zero. This helps reduce the model's sensitivity to specific inputs.

TensorFlow allows you to apply these regularizations using the class regularizers. Below is the definition of a model with L1 and L2 regularization:

python

```python
from tensorflow.keras.regularizers import l1, l2

# Model with L1 and L2 regularization
model = Sequential([
    Dense(units=128, activation='relu',
kernel_regularizer=l1(0.01), input_shape=(100,)),
    Dense(units=64, activation='relu',
kernel_regularizer=l2(0.01)),
    Dense(units=10, activation='softmax')
])

# Compiling the model
model.compile(
    optimizer='adam',
    loss='sparse_categorical_crossentropy',
```

```
    metrics=['accuracy']
)

# Model summary
model.summary()
```

In the example above, the hyperparameters l1 and l2 control the intensity of regularization. Higher values increase the penalty, forcing smaller weights.

python

```
# Training the model
model.fit(X_train, y_train, epochs=10, batch_size=32)
```

L2 regularization is widely used as a default in many implementations due to its stability and efficiency. L1, on the other hand, is useful in situations where a sparser model is needed.

Combination of Regularization Techniques

It is common to combine several regularization techniques to maximize model generalization. An example model that uses Dropout and L2 regularization:

python

```
model = Sequential([
    Dense(units=128, activation='relu',
kernel_regularizer=l2(0.01), input_shape=(100,)),
    Dropout(rate=0.4),
    Dense(units=64, activation='relu',
kernel_regularizer=l2(0.01)),
    Dropout(rate=0.2),
    Dense(units=10, activation='softmax')
])

model.compile(
    optimizer='adam',
```

```
    loss='sparse_categorical_crossentropy',
    metrics=['accuracy']
)

# Training the model
model.fit(X_train, y_train, epochs=10, batch_size=32)
```

Combining Dropout and penalties helps create more robust models, especially in complex problems.

Regularization with Augmented Data

Another effective approach to reducing overfitting is data augmentation, which artificially increases the size of the dataset. In computer vision, augmentation can include operations such as rotation, translation and inversion of images.

In TensorFlow, augmentation can be applied using specific layers such as RandomFlip and RandomRotation:

python

```
from tensorflow.keras.layers import RandomFlip,
RandomRotation

# Creating an augmentation pipeline
data_augmentation = Sequential([
    RandomFlip("horizontal"),
    RandomRotation(0.1)
])

# Applying augmentation to a model
model = Sequential([
    data_augmentation,
    Dense(units=128, activation='relu',
kernel_regularizer=l2(0.01)),
    Dense(units=64, activation='relu',
kernel_regularizer=l2(0.01)),
    Dense(units=10, activation='softmax')
])
```

```
model.compile(
    optimizer='adam',
    loss='sparse_categorical_crossentropy',
    metrics=['accuracy']
)
```

Data augmentation is particularly effective on small data sets, where the model can learn unwanted patterns.

Overfitting Monitoring

To evaluate the effectiveness of regularization techniques, it is essential to monitor model performance on training and validation data. A large difference between training and validation metrics may indicate overfitting.

python

```
history = model.fit(X_train, y_train, validation_split=0.2,
epochs=20, batch_size=32)

# Plotting performance
import matplotlib.pyplot as plt

plt.plot(history.history['accuracy'], label='Treinamento')
plt.plot(history.history['val_accuracy'], label='Validação')
plt.xlabel('Épocas')
plt.ylabel('Accuracy')
plt.legend()
plt.show()
```

Regularization helps minimize this discrepancy, improving the model's ability to generalize to new data.

Regularization techniques are essential for the development of robust and generalizable neural networks. Methods like Dropout, L1, and L2 reduce the risk of overfitting, while complementary approaches like data augmentation increase the diversity of the training set. By combining these strategies, it is possible to create models that balance complexity and precision, delivering reliable results in different scenarios.

CHAPTER 9: DATASETS AND PIPELINES WITH TF.DATA

Efficient data handling is essential in deep learning, especially when working with large volumes of information. The module tf.data TensorFlow provides tools for creating and managing robust and scalable data pipelines. With it, you can load, process, transform and feed models efficiently. Creating well-structured pipelines improves performance and generalization, ensuring data is utilized optimally during training.

Creation of Datasets with tf.data

THE tf.data.Dataset is the main class for working with data in TensorFlow. It allows you to create datasets from different sources, such as lists, arrays, CSV files or images. To create a dataset from tensors or arrays:

python

```
import tensorflow as tf

# Creating a dataset from lists
data = [1, 2, 3, 4, 5]
dataset = tf.data.Dataset.from_tensor_slices(data)

# Iterating over the dataset
for element in dataset:
    print(element.numpy())
```

The method from_tensor_slices splits data into individual elements, allowing batch processing later.

When working with tabular data, the tf.data.experimental.make_csv_dataset simplifies reading and transforming CSV files:

python

```
# Creating a dataset from a CSV file
csv_file = "data.csv" # Replace with CSV file path
csv_dataset = tf.data.experimental.make_csv_dataset(
    csv_file,
    batch_size=32,
    num_epochs=1,
    shuffle=True
)

# Displaying batches of the dataset
for batch in csv_dataset:
    print(batch)
```

This method reads CSV files and organizes the data into batches ready for training.

Dataset Manipulation and Transformation

THE tf.data offers operations to flexibly transform datasets. One of the most common operations is mapping, which applies a function to each element of the dataset:

python

```
# Transforming dataset elements
def transform_fn(x):
    return x * 2

transformed_dataset = dataset.map(transform_fn)

# Displaying the transformed dataset
for element in transformed_dataset:
    print(element.numpy())
```

Mapping is especially useful for normalizing, standardizing, or fine-tuning data before training.

Another fundamental operation is grouping elements into batches. This allows the model to process multiple examples at once:

python

```
# Splitting the dataset into batches
batched_dataset = dataset.batch(2)

# Iterating batch hairs
for batch in batched_dataset:
    print(batch.numpy())
```

Data shuffling is also essential to prevent unwanted patterns in the dataset from influencing learning:

python

```
# Shuffling the data
shuffled_dataset = dataset.shuffle(buffer_size=5)

# Displaying the shuffled dataset
for element in shuffled_dataset:
    print(element.numpy())
```

Data Augmentation Techniques

Data augmentation is an effective technique to artificially increase the size of the dataset by introducing variations in the original data. In computer vision, it is used to create images modified by rotation, flipping, changing brightness, or cropping. TensorFlow offers dedicated layers for augmentation:

python

```
from tensorflow.keras.layers import RandomFlip,
```

```
RandomRotation

# Creating an augmentation pipeline
data_augmentation = tf.keras.Sequential([
    RandomFlip("horizontal"),
    RandomRotation(0.1)
])

# Applying augmentation to a batch of images
images = tf.random.normal([4, 128, 128, 3]) # 4 128x128 images
with 3 channels
augmented_images = data_augmentation(images)

# Displaying the dimensions of the processed batch
print(augmented_images.shape)
```

These transformations are applied dynamically during training, ensuring greater diversity without the need to alter the original data.

Data Preprocessing with tf.data

Preprocessing is essential to prepare data before training. This includes normalization, category coding, and converting data into model-compatible formats.

Normalization standardizes data to a specific range, such as 0 to 1:

python

```
# Normalizing values between 0 and 1
def normalize_fn(x):
    return x / 255.0

normalized_dataset = dataset.map(normalize_fn)

for element in normalized_dataset:
    print(element.numpy())
```

Category encoding converts categorical values into numeric

representations or one-hot encoding:

python

```
# Encoding categories with one-hot encoding
def one_hot_fn(x):
    return tf.one_hot(x, depth=5)

one_hot_dataset = dataset.map(one_hot_fn)

for element in one_hot_dataset:
    print(element.numpy())
```

Standardization is another common technique, especially when dealing with continuous numeric input:

python

```
# Standardizing values
def standardize_fn(x):
    mean, std = tf.reduce_mean(x), tf.math.reduce_std(x)
    return (x - mean) / std

standardized_dataset = dataset.map(standardize_fn)

for element in standardized_dataset:
    print(element.numpy())
```

Integration with Models

The datasets created and processed with tf.data can be directly integrated into model training in TensorFlow. The method fit accepts objects Dataset as input:

python

```
from tensorflow.keras import Sequential
from tensorflow.keras.layers import Dense

# Creating a simple model
model = Sequential([
```

```
    Dense(units=64, activation='relu', input_shape=(1,)),
    Dense(units=1, activation='linear')
])

# Compiling the model
model.compile(optimizer='adam', loss='mse')

# Training the model with a dataset
model.fit(dataset.batch(32), epochs=10)
```

By integrating data pipelines with tf.data, data is loaded and processed efficiently during training.

Advanced Pipelines with prefetch and cache

To improve performance, tf.data allows the execution of data preload and cache operations. The method prefetch performs operations in parallel with training, minimizing bottlenecks:

python

```
# Adding prefetch to the pipeline
optimized_dataset =
dataset.batch(32).prefetch(buffer_size=tf.data.experimental.AU
TOTUNE)

# Training the model with the optimized dataset
model.fit(optimized_dataset, epochs=10)
```

The method cache stores processed data in memory or on disk, speeding up subsequent iterations:

python

```
# Caching the dataset
cached_dataset = dataset.batch(32).cache()

# Training the model
model.fit(cached_dataset, epochs=10)
```

The use of tf.data for manipulating and creating data

pipelines transforms the way data is prepared for training deep learning models. The combination of efficiency, flexibility, and support for advanced techniques such as augmentation and preprocessing allows developers to create robust, scalable solutions to handle large volumes of data in a variety of formats. This approach ensures that data is processed and used optimally, improving the overall performance of the models.

CHAPTER 10: CONVOLUTIONAL NETWORKS (CNNS)

Convolutional Neural Networks (CNNs) have revolutionized the field of computer vision. Designed to process data with spatial structures such as images and videos, CNNs are highly effective at identifying visual patterns such as edges, textures and shapes. This chapter explores the fundamentals of CNNs, their practical applications in computer vision, and the implementation of image classifiers using TensorFlow.

Fundamentals of Convolutional Networks

CNNs are made up of specialized layers that perform operations such as convolution, pooling, and normalization. These layers work together to learn hierarchical representations of input data, starting with basic features and evolving to more complex patterns.

Structure of a CNN

A typical CNN is made up of the following layers:

1. **Convolutional Layers**
   They perform the convolution operation, applying filters (kernels) to detect local features in the input data.

python

```
from tensorflow.keras.layers import Conv2D

# Creating a convolutional layer

conv_layer = Conv2D(filters=32, kernel_size=(3, 3),
activation='relu', input_shape=(128, 128, 3))
```

2. **Pooling Layers**
   They reduce the dimensionality of the data, maintaining the most important characteristics. The most common pooling is max pooling.

python

```
from tensorflow.keras.layers import MaxPooling2D

# Creating a pooling layer

pool_layer = MaxPooling2D(pool_size=(2, 2))
```

3. **Flatten and Dense Layers**
   The Flatten layer converts the features into a vector, and the dense layers perform classification based on these features.

python

```
from tensorflow.keras.layers import Flatten, Dense

# Creating Flatten and Dense layers

flatten_layer = Flatten()

dense_layer = Dense(units=128, activation='relu')
```

Image Processing with CNNs

Images have spatial properties and local relationships that make

CNNs particularly effective. Convolution is an operation that exploits these properties, learning patterns in small pieces of the image.

Convolution Operation

The convolution operation involves applying a kernel (filter) to the input, producing a feature map. Filters learn specific features, such as horizontal, vertical, or diagonal edges.

Pooling

Pooling is a dimensionality reduction technique that consolidates information into regions of the image. Max pooling selects the maximum value in a region, while average pooling calculates the average.

python

```
import tensorflow as tf


# Max pooling example

input_tensor = tf.constant([[[1, 2], [3, 4]], [[5, 6], [7, 8]]], dtype=tf.float32)

pooled_tensor = tf.nn.max_pool2d(input_tensor[tf.newaxis, ..., tf.newaxis], ksize=2, strides=1, padding='VALID')

print(pooled_tensor.numpy())
```

Practical Implementation of Image Classifiers

CNNs are widely used for image classification, such as categorizing objects in a photo or facial recognition. Below, the practical implementation of an image classifier with TensorFlow using the CIFAR-10 dataset, which contains 60,000 images in 10 categories, is presented.

Dataset Configuration

The CIFAR-10 dataset can be loaded directly from TensorFlow:

python

```
from tensorflow.keras.datasets import cifar10
from tensorflow.keras.utils import to_categorical

# Loading the dataset
(X_train, y_train), (X_test, y_test) = cifar10.load_data()

# Normalizing the images
X_train = X_train / 255.0
X_test = X_test / 255.0

# Converting labels to one-hot encoding
y_train = to_categorical(y_train, 10)
y_test = to_categorical(y_test, 10)
```

Model Construction

The model will be a CNN with several convolutional, pooling and dense layers.

python

```
from tensorflow.keras.models import Sequential
```

```
from tensorflow.keras.layers import Conv2D, MaxPooling2D,
Flatten, Dense, Dropout


# Creating the model
model = Sequential([
    Conv2D(32, (3, 3), activation='relu', input_shape=(32, 32, 3)),
    MaxPooling2D((2, 2)),
    Conv2D(64, (3, 3), activation='relu'),
    MaxPooling2D((2, 2)),
    Conv2D(128, (3, 3), activation='relu'),
    Flatten(),
    Dense(128, activation='relu'),
    Dropout(0.5),
    Dense(10, activation='softmax')  # 10 classes no CIFAR-10
])
```

Model Compilation and Training

After creating the model, configure the optimizer, loss function, and metrics for training.

python

```
model.compile(optimizer='adam',
loss='categorical_crossentropy', metrics=['accuracy'])


# Training the model
history = model.fit(X_train, y_train, epochs=20, batch_size=64,
validation_data=(X_test, y_test))
```

Assessment and Inference

Evaluate model performance on the test set and use it to make inferences.

python

```
# Model evaluation
test_loss, test_accuracy = model.evaluate(X_test, y_test)
print(f"Test accuracy: {test_accuracy}")

# Making predictions
predictions = model.predict(X_test[:5])
print(predictions)
```

Advanced Applications of CNNs

In addition to simple classifiers, CNNs are used in more complex tasks, such as object detection, image segmentation and image generation.

Object Detection

In object detection, the goal is to locate and identify different objects in an image. Architectures like YOLO and Faster R-CNN are widely used.

Image Segmentation

Segmentation divides the image into different regions or objects. Networks such as U-Net and Mask R-CNN are examples of architectures for this task.

Image Generation

Generative adversarial networks (GANs) use CNNs to create realistic images, widely applied in areas such as design and entertainment.

Best Practices for CNNs

1. **Hyperparameter Tuning**
   Test different filter sizes, dropout rates, and activation functions to find the best configuration.
2. **Data Augmentation**
   Augment the dataset with techniques such as rotation, mirroring and cropping to improve generalization.

python

```
from tensorflow.keras.preprocessing.image import
ImageDataGenerator


# Configuring data augmentation

datagen = ImageDataGenerator(rotation_range=20,
horizontal_flip=True, width_shift_range=0.2,
height_shift_range=0.2)

datagen.fit(X_train)
```

3. **Regularization**
   Use dropout and normalization to avoid overfitting.
4. **Distributed Training**
   Use multiple GPUs to speed up training on large datasets.

AConvolutional Networks are a fundamental pillar of

computer vision, enabling accurate and efficient solutions for tasks ranging from image classification to generation and segmentation. Mastering its bases, understanding its applications and implementing practical projects opens doors to exploring the limits of artificial intelligence and creating systems that positively impact different sectors.

CHAPTER 11: RECURRENT NETWORKS (RNNS)

Recurrent Neural Networks (RNNs) are architectures designed to process sequential and time-series data such as text, audio signals, financial data, and other order-dependent information. Unlike traditional neural networks, RNNs have the ability to "remember" previous information, which makes them ideal for dealing with sequences of data. This chapter explores the fundamental structures of RNNs, including LSTMs and GRUs, their practical applications, and implementation in TensorFlow.

Structure of Recurrent Networks (RNNs)

RNNs are based on recurrent connections, which allow the output of a neuron at a given time to be used as input for the same neuron at the next time. This creates a kind of memory, allowing the network to analyze temporal relationships in the data.

How RNNs Process Sequences

Instead of processing inputs independently, as in dense networks, RNNs process inputs sequentially, conveying information through hidden states. The basic architecture consists of the following components:

1. **Sequential Input**
   Each element of the sequence is fed into the network in

time steps.

2. **Hidden State**
   The hidden state is updated at each step based on the current input and the previous state.
3. **Sequential or Single Output**
   Output can be generated at each step (for tasks like language translation) or just at the end of the sequence (for tasks like text classification).

python

```
import tensorflow as tf

# Creating a simple RNN layer
rnn_layer = tf.keras.layers.SimpleRNN(32, input_shape=(10, 8))
# 10 time steps, 8 features per step
```

Problems with Classical RNNs

Although basic RNNs are powerful, they have significant limitations, such as:

- **Vanishing and Exploding Gradients**
  During training, gradients can become too small or too large, making it difficult to update weights and hindering long-term dependency learning.
- **Limited Memory**
  Classical RNNs have difficulty capturing long-range information in sequences.

These problems have led to the development of advanced architectures such as LSTMs and GRUs.

LSTMs (Long Short-Term Memory)

LSTMs were designed to overcome the limitations of classical

RNNs by introducing more sophisticated memory mechanisms. They use memory cells, input ports, forget ports, and output ports to manage information more effectively.

LSTM components

1. **Memory Cell**
   Stores relevant information over time.
2. **Entry Door**
   Decides which input information should be stored in the memory cell.
3. **Door of Oblivion**
   Determines what information should be discarded.
4. **Exit Port**
   Controls which memory cell information will be used to calculate the output.

python

```
# Creating an LSTM layer
lstm_layer = tf.keras.layers.LSTM(64, input_shape=(10, 8)) # 10
time steps, 8 features per step
```

LSTM applications

LSTMs are widely used in tasks such as:

- Natural language processing (NLP), including sentiment analysis and machine translation.
- Forecasting time series such as stock prices and energy consumption.
- Speech recognition and audio signal processing.

GRUs (Gated Recurrent Units)

GRUs are a simplification of LSTMs, with fewer parameters and less computational complexity. They combine the input port and the forget port into a single update port.

Advantages of GRUs

- Lower computational cost due to the reduction of components.
- Performance comparable to LSTMs in many tasks.

python

```
# Creating a GRU layer
gru_layer = tf.keras.layers.GRU(64, input_shape=(10, 8)) # 10
time steps, 8 features per step
```

GRU applications

GRUs are used in similar scenarios to LSTMs, especially when there are resource constraints or model simplicity is a priority.

Time Series and Sequence Processing

RNNs, LSTMs and GRUs are widely applied in processing time series and sequences. Below we explore some of the main applications.

Time Series Forecasting

A common application is predicting future values based on historical patterns, such as forecast demand, market prices, and weather conditions.

python

```
# Creating a model for time series forecasting
model = tf.keras.Sequential([
    tf.keras.layers.LSTM(64, return_sequences=True,
input_shape=(30, 1)), # 30 time steps, 1 feature
    tf.keras.layers.LSTM(32),
    tf.keras.layers.Dense(1) # Single value prediction
])

model.compile(optimizer='adam', loss='mse')
```

Sentiment Analysis

Another use is to analyze sentiments in texts, classifying messages as positive, negative or neutral.

python

```
# Creating an LSTM model for sentiment analysis
model = tf.keras.Sequential([
    tf.keras.layers.Embedding(input_dim=5000,
output_dim=64, input_length=100),  # 5000 palavras no
vocabulário
    tf.keras.layers.LSTM(128),
    tf.keras.layers.Dense(1, activation='sigmoid') # Binary output
])

model.compile(optimizer='adam', loss='binary_crossentropy',
metrics=['accuracy'])
```

Machine Translation

In language translation, RNNs are used in encoder-decoder architectures, where one model encodes the input sequence into a vector and another model decodes it to produce the translation.

Techniques to Improve Performance

When working with RNNs, LSTMs, and GRUs, there are strategies that can improve model performance and efficiency.

Regularization

Add Dropout to avoid overfitting and improve generalization.

python

```python
# Using Dropout in an LSTM
model = tf.keras.Sequential([
    tf.keras.layers.LSTM(64, return_sequences=True,
dropout=0.2, input_shape=(30, 1)),
    tf.keras.layers.LSTM(32, dropout=0.2),
    tf.keras.layers.Dense(1)
])
```

Hyperparameter Tuning

Experiment with different layer sizes, learning rates, and activation functions to find the best configuration for the problem.

Training on Long Data

Use sequence truncation to handle very long sequences by breaking them into smaller, more manageable parts.

Recurrent Neural Networks, together with LSTMs and GRUs, offer powerful solutions to a wide range of problems involving sequential and time series data. With their ability to model temporal dependencies and complex relationships, these networks play a crucial role in areas such as natural language processing, time series analysis, and pattern recognition in sequences. Mastering these techniques opens doors to solving complex problems with creativity and precision.

CHAPTER 12: TRANSFER LEARNING

Transfer learning, or Transfer Learning, is an approach that allows you to take advantage of the knowledge acquired by pre-trained models on large datasets to solve specific problems with less data and less training time. Instead of training a model from scratch, this technique reuses networks already trained on related tasks such as image classification or text processing. This method is widely used in deep learning due to its efficiency and effectiveness, especially in scenarios with limited resources or small datasets.

Introduction to Reusing Pre-trained Models

Pre-trained models are networks that have already undergone extensive training on large and diverse datasets, such as ImageNet, which contains millions of images categorized into thousands of classes. These models learn to identify general patterns, such as edges, shapes, and textures, which are useful in many visual tasks. By reusing them, time and computational resources are saved, as well as improving performance in problems with limited data.

Popular models include:

- **VGG**: Focused on simplicity and depth with stacked convolutional layers.
- **ResNet**: Introduces residual connections, which help train very deep networks.
- **MobileNet**: Designed for efficiency on mobile devices.

- **BERT** and **GPT**: Widely used in natural language processing.

In TensorFlow, these models can be easily accessed through the module tf.keras.applications.

Using Pre-trained Models

To use a pre-trained model, load the architecture with the trained weights and adapt it to the desired task. For example, VGG16 can be used as a basis for image classification:

python

```
from tensorflow.keras.applications import VGG16
from tensorflow.keras import Sequential
from tensorflow.keras.layers import Dense, Flatten

# Loading pre-trained VGG16 model
base_model = VGG16(weights='imagenet', include_top=False,
input_shape=(224, 224, 3))

# Freezing base model weights
base_model.trainable = False

# Creating a new model with VGG16 as a base
model = Sequential([
    base_model,
    Flatten(),
    Dense(256, activation='relu'),
    Dense(10, activation='softmax') # Output for 10 classes
])

# Model summary
model.summary()
```

In this case, VGG16 convolutional layers are used to extract features from images, while new dense layers are added to perform specific classification.

Compilation and Training

After building the model, you need to compile it with an optimizer, a loss function, and appropriate metrics. In multi-class classification problems, the loss function sparse_categorical_crossentropy is often used:

python

```
# Compiling the model
model.compile(
    optimizer='adam',
    loss='sparse_categorical_crossentropy',
    metrics=['accuracy']
)

# Loading training and validation data
train_dataset = tf.keras.utils.image_dataset_from_directory(
    'path_to_train_data',
    image_size=(224, 224),
    batch_size=32
)

val_dataset = tf.keras.utils.image_dataset_from_directory(
    'path_to_val_data',
    image_size=(224, 224),
    batch_size=32
)

# Training the model
model.fit(train_dataset, validation_data=val_dataset,
epochs=10)
```

Freezing pre-trained layers prevents their weights from changing during training, preserving the knowledge gained.

Fine-tuning for Specific Problems

Fine-tuning is an additional step in Transfer Learning where some or all layers of the pre-trained model are adjusted to the new problem. This technique is particularly useful when the target dataset is substantially different from the original dataset used to train the model.

To perform Fine-tuning, unfreeze the desired layers before recompiling and training the model:

python

```
# Making convolutional layers trainable
base_model.trainable = True

# Compiling the model again
model.compile(
    optimizer=tf.keras.optimizers.Adam(learning_rate=1e-5),
    loss='sparse_categorical_crossentropy',
    metrics=['accuracy']
)

# Training with Fine-tuning
model.fit(train_dataset, validation_data=val_dataset,
epochs=5)
```

Reducing the learning rate is crucial to avoid large changes in pre-trained weights.

Advantages and Limitations of Transfer Learning

Advantages:

- **Saving time and resources**: Reusing a pre-trained model significantly reduces the computational cost.
- **Performance improvement**: Models start with well-tuned weights, which generally leads to better results on small datasets.
- **Flexibility**: It can be applied to various tasks, from computer vision to natural language processing.

Limitations:

- **Dependency on the original dataset**: Performance may be limited if the original dataset is very different from the target dataset.
- **Complexity in Fine-tuning**: Adjusting layers without over-adjusting can be challenging.

Using Pre-trained Models for Other Tasks

In addition to image classification, Transfer Learning can be used in tasks such as object detection and image segmentation. For example, the pre-trained Mask R-CNN model is widely used for instance segmentation, while YOLO (You Only Look Once) is a popular option for real-time object detection.

Transfer Learning in Natural Language Processing (NLP)

In NLP, models like BERT and GPT are widely used for tasks like sentiment analysis, question answering, and machine translation. TensorFlow supports these models through the module transformers.

python

```
from transformers import TFBertForSequenceClassification,
BertTokenizer

# Loading the BERT model and tokenizer
model =
TFBertForSequenceClassification.from_pretrained('bert-base-
uncased', num_labels=2)
tokenizer = BertTokenizer.from_pretrained('bert-base-uncased')

# Tokenizing text
inputs = tokenizer("The movie was fantastic!",
return_tensors="tf")
```

```
# Making a prediction
outputs = model(inputs)
print(outputs)
```

Hyperparameter Monitoring and Tuning

Monitoring the model's performance during training is essential to ensure it is not overfitting or underfitting the data. Tools like TensorBoard can be integrated to track metrics:

python

```
# Configuring TensorBoard
tensorboard_callback =
tf.keras.callbacks.TensorBoard(log_dir="./logs")

# Training the model with callback
model.fit(train_dataset, validation_data=val_dataset,
epochs=10, callbacks=[tensorboard_callback])
```

Tuning hyperparameters like learning rate, number of trainable layers, and batch size can further improve model performance.

Transfer Learning is a powerful technique that democratizes the use of deep learning, enabling even teams with limited resources to achieve advanced results. Repurposing pre-trained models reduces development time, improves efficiency, and provides a solid starting point for solving specific problems. Combined with Fine-tuning, this approach maximizes performance and versatility, making it a must-have in the arsenal of any deep learning developer or researcher.

CHAPTER 13: GENERATIVE ADVERSARIAL NETWORKS (GANS)

Generative Adversarial Networks (GANs) are a revolutionary approach in the field of deep learning, allowing models to generate new data with characteristics similar to real data. These networks are composed of two models: a generator and a discriminator, which compete with each other to continually improve. GANs have diverse applications, such as generating realistic images, creating art, data augmentation, and image reconstruction.

Construction and Operation of GANs

GANs are made up of two main parts:

1. **Generator**: A model that learns to create data from random noise. It tries to produce samples that are indistinguishable from the real data to fool the discriminator.
2. **Discriminator**: A model that attempts to distinguish between real data and data generated by the generator. It is essentially a binary classifier, trained to identify whether a sample is real or fake.

Training a GAN occurs in a competition cycle. The generator tries to improve its ability to fool the discriminator, while the discriminator tries to improve its ability to identify the generated samples.

Building a GAN with TensorFlow

TensorFlow offers powerful tools for building and training GANs. Below is the implementation of a GAN for generating simple images, such as handwritten digits from the MNIST dataset.

Data Preparation

First, load the MNIST dataset and normalize the pixel values to the range between -1 and 1, necessary for training stability:

python

```
import tensorflow as tf
from tensorflow.keras.datasets import mnist

# Loading the MNIST dataset
(train_images, _), (_, _) = mnist.load_data()

# Normalizing the data
train_images = train_images.reshape(train_images.shape[0], 28,
28, 1).astype('float32')
train_images = (train_images - 127.5) / 127.5 # Normalizing to
the range [-1, 1]

# Creating batches
BUFFER_SIZE = 60000
BATCH_SIZE = 256

dataset =
tf.data.Dataset.from_tensor_slices(train_images).shuffle(BUFFE
R_SIZE).batch(BATCH_SIZE)
```

Generator Construction

The generator is a model that transforms random noise into

images. It uses transposed convolution layers to generate data with the correct structure.

python

```
from tensorflow.keras import Sequential
from tensorflow.keras.layers import Dense, Reshape,
Conv2DTranspose, BatchNormalization, ReLU

def build_generator():
    model = Sequential([
        Dense(7 * 7 * 256, use_bias=False, input_shape=(100,)),
        BatchNormalization(),
        ReLU(),
        Reshape((7, 7, 256)),
        Conv2DTranspose(128, (5, 5), strides=(1, 1),
padding='same', use_bias=False),
        BatchNormalization(),
        ReLU(),
        Conv2DTranspose(64, (5, 5), strides=(2, 2),
padding='same', use_bias=False),
        BatchNormalization(),
        ReLU(),
        Conv2DTranspose(1, (5, 5), strides=(2, 2), padding='same',
use_bias=False, activation='tanh')
    ])
    return model

generator = build_generator()
generator.summary()
```

The generator starts with a noise input (100-dimensional vector) and expands it to form a 28x28 image with a single channel.

Construction of the Discriminator

The discriminator is a model that classifies images as real or fake. It uses convolutional layers to extract features from images.

python

```
from tensorflow.keras.layers import Flatten, LeakyReLU,
Dropout

def build_discriminator():
    model = Sequential([
        Conv2DTranspose(64, (5, 5), strides=(2, 2),
padding='same', input_shape=[28, 28, 1]),
        LeakyReLU(alpha=0.2),
        Dropout(0.3),
        Flatten(),
        Dense(1, activation='sigmoid')
    ])
    return model

discriminator = build_discriminator()
discriminator.summary()
```

The discriminator returns a value between 0 and 1, representing the probability that the image is real.

Compilation and Losses

GANs use specific loss functions to train the generator and discriminator. The generator loss is based on its ability to fool the discriminator, while the discriminator loss measures its accuracy in distinguishing real from generated data.

python

```
from tensorflow.keras.optimizers import Adam

# Loss functions
cross_entropy =
tf.keras.losses.BinaryCrossentropy(from_logits=True)

def generator_loss(fake_output):
    return cross_entropy(tf.ones_like(fake_output),
```

```
fake_output)

def discriminator_loss(real_output, fake_output):
    real_loss = cross_entropy(tf.ones_like(real_output),
real_output)
    fake_loss = cross_entropy(tf.zeros_like(fake_output),
fake_output)
    return real_loss + fake_loss

# Optimizers
generator_optimizer = Adam(1e-4)
discriminator_optimizer = Adam(1e-4)
```

Training

Training occurs in cycles, where the generator and discriminator are trained alternately.

python

```
import numpy as np

EPOCHS = 50
NOISE_DIM = 100
NUM_EXAMPLES = 16

seed = tf.random.normal([NUM_EXAMPLES, NOISE_DIM])

@tf.function
def train_step(images):
    noise = tf.random.normal([BATCH_SIZE, NOISE_DIM])

    with tf.GradientTape() as gen_tape, tf.GradientTape() as
disc_tape:
        generated_images = generator(noise, training=True)

        real_output = discriminator(images, training=True)
        fake_output = discriminator(generated_images,
training=True)

        gen_loss = generator_loss(fake_output)
```

```
        disc_loss = discriminator_loss(real_output, fake_output)

    gradients_of_generator = gen_tape.gradient(gen_loss,
generator.trainable_variables)
    gradients_of_discriminator = disc_tape.gradient(disc_loss,
discriminator.trainable_variables)

    generator_optimizer.apply_gradients(zip(gradients_of_gene
rator, generator.trainable_variables))
    discriminator_optimizer.apply_gradients(zip(gradients_of_d
iscriminator, discriminator.trainable_variables))

def train(dataset, epochs):
    for epoch in range(epochs):
        for image_batch in dataset:
            train_step(image_batch)
```

Image Generation

After training, the generator can create realistic images from noise.

python

```
import matplotlib.pyplot as plt

def generate_and_save_images(model, epoch, test_input):
    predictions = model(test_input, training=False)
    fig = plt.figure(figsize=(4, 4))

    for i in range(predictions.shape[0]):
        plt.subplot(4, 4, i + 1)
        plt.imshow((predictions[i, :, :, 0] + 1) / 2, cmap='gray')
        plt.axis('off')

    plt.show()

generate_and_save_images(generator, 0, seed)
```

GANs are powerful tools that push the limits of what

neural networks can achieve. They allow you to create new realistic data and have applications in various fields, from art to medicine. Building and training a GAN requires a careful understanding of the balance between generator and discriminator, but the rewards in terms of innovation and results are incomparable. By mastering this technology, developers can explore new horizons in deep learning.

CHAPTER 14: TRANSFORMERS

Transformers are one of the biggest innovations in deep learning, revolutionizing natural language processing (NLP) and other areas. Introduced as an architecture that replaces recurrent and convolutional networks in sequence tasks, Transformers use attention mechanisms to capture relationships between words or elements in a sequence, regardless of the distance between them. Transformer-based models like BERT and GPT have transformed the way we understand and process language, enabling advances in machine translation, text generation, sentiment analysis, and other tasks.

Transformers Fundamentals

Transformers operates on three main concepts:

1. **Attention Mechanism**
   The attention mechanism allows Transformers to assign different weights to words or tokens in a sequence based on their relevance to the current context. This solves the limitation of models such as recurrent networks, which had difficulty capturing long-range relationships in sequences.
2. **Parallel Representations**
   While recurrent networks process sequences sequentially, Transformers process all tokens simultaneously. This parallel approach significantly

improves performance on accelerated hardware such as GPUs and TPUs.

3. **Encoders and Decoders**
   The original Transformers architecture is made up of two main components:
   - THE **encoder**, which reads input and creates internal representations.
   - THE **decoder**, which uses these representations to generate an output.

Although the original architecture is bidirectional, models like GPT only use the decoder part for text generation.

Building a Transformer with TensorFlow

TensorFlow provides libraries and tools for building and training Transformers. A basic implementation includes attention and encoding layers.

Attention Layer

Attention is central to the functioning of Transformers. Below is an implementation of scaled attention in TensorFlow:

python

```
import tensorflow as tf

def scaled_dot_product_attention(query, key, value,
mask=None):
    matmul_qk = tf.matmul(query, key, transpose_b=True)
    dk = tf.cast(tf.shape(key)[-1], tf.float32)
    scaled_attention_logits = matmul_qk / tf.math.sqrt(dk)

    if mask is not None:
        scaled_attention_logits += (mask * -1e9)

    attention_weights = tf.nn.softmax(scaled_attention_logits,
axis=-1)
```

```
    output = tf.matmul(attention_weights, value)
    return output, attention_weights
```

Multi-Head Attention

Transformers utilize multiple attention heads to allow the model to focus on different parts of the sequence at the same time:

python

```
from tensorflow.keras.layers import Dense

class MultiHeadAttention(tf.keras.layers.Layer):
    def __init__(self, d_model, num_heads):
        super(MultiHeadAttention, self).__init__()
        self.num_heads = num_heads
        self.d_model = d_model

        assert d_model % self.num_heads == 0

        self.depth = d_model // self.num_heads
        self.wq = Dense(d_model)
        self.wk = Dense(d_model)
        self.wv = Dense(d_model)
        self.dense = Dense(d_model)

    def split_heads(self, x, batch_size):
        x = tf.reshape(x, (batch_size, -1, self.num_heads,
self.depth))
        return tf.transpose(x, perm=[0, 2, 1, 3])

    def call(self, query, key, value, mask):
        batch_size = tf.shape(query)[0]
        query = self.split_heads(self.wq(query), batch_size)
        key = self.split_heads(self.wk(key), batch_size)
        value = self.split_heads(self.wv(value), batch_size)

        attention, _ = scaled_dot_product_attention(query, key,
value, mask)
```

```
        attention = tf.transpose(attention, perm=[0, 2, 1, 3])
        concat_attention = tf.reshape(attention, (batch_size, -1,
self.d_model))
        return self.dense(concat_attention)
```

Transformer Encoder

The encoder applies attention in conjunction with feedforward and normalization layers:

python

```
class TransformerEncoderLayer(tf.keras.layers.Layer):
    def __init__(self, d_model, num_heads, dff, rate=0.1):
        super(TransformerEncoderLayer, self).__init__()
        self.mha = MultiHeadAttention(d_model, num_heads)
        self.ffn = tf.keras.Sequential([
            Dense(dff, activation='relu'),
            Dense(d_model)
        ])
        self.layernorm1 =
tf.keras.layers.LayerNormalization(epsilon=1e-6)
        self.layernorm2 =
tf.keras.layers.LayerNormalization(epsilon=1e-6)
        self.dropout1 = tf.keras.layers.Dropout(rate)
        self.dropout2 = tf.keras.layers.Dropout(rate)

    def call(self, x, training, mask):
        attn_output = self.mha(x, x, x, mask)
        attn_output = self.dropout1(attn_output,
training=training)
        out1 = self.layernorm1(x + attn_output)
        ffn_output = self.ffn(out1)
        ffn_output = self.dropout2(ffn_output, training=training)
        return self.layernorm2(out1 + ffn_output)
```

Application with Pre-trained Models: BERT and GPT

BERT and GPT are two of the best-known models based on Transformers. TensorFlow offers libraries to use them easily, such as transformers.

Loading BERT for Classification

BERT (Bidirectional Encoder Representations from Transformers) is widely used in NLP for tasks like sentiment analysis and text classification:

python

```
from transformers import TFBertForSequenceClassification,
BertTokenizer

# Loading the BERT model and tokenizer
model =
TFBertForSequenceClassification.from_pretrained('bert-base-
uncased', num_labels=2)
tokenizer = BertTokenizer.from_pretrained('bert-base-uncased')

# Tokenizing text
inputs = tokenizer("The movie was fantastic!",
return_tensors="tf")

# Making a prediction
outputs = model(inputs)
print(outputs.logits)
```

Loading GPT for Text Generation

GPT (Generative Pre-trained Transformer) is used for continuous text generation:

python

```
from transformers import TFGPT2LMHeadModel,
GPT2Tokenizer

# Loading the GPT model and tokenizer
model = TFGPT2LMHeadModel.from_pretrained('gpt2')
tokenizer = GPT2Tokenizer.from_pretrained('gpt2')

# Text generation
input_text = "Once upon a time"
input_ids = tokenizer.encode(input_text, return_tensors='tf')
output = model.generate(input_ids, max_length=50,
num_return_sequences=1)
print(tokenizer.decode(output[0], skip_special_tokens=True))
```

Impact Two Transformers

Transformers revolutionized NLP by introducing an efficient and scalable approach to modeling sequences. They resolved significant limitations of recurrent networks, such as difficulty in capturing long-range relationships and high computational demand. In addition to NLP, Transformers are being adapted for computer vision, bioinformatics and other emerging areas.

Transformers are a key player in advancing deep learning, redefining the state of the art in various tasks. With their flexible architecture and superior performance, they continue to open up new possibilities, enabling researchers and developers to address complex problems more effectively. Mastering the concepts and practical implementations of Transformers is essential for anyone looking to explore the potential of deep learning in 2024 and beyond.

CHAPTER 15: VISUALIZATION WITH TENSORBOARD

TensorBoard is an essential tool for monitoring and visualizing the training of deep learning models in real time. It allows developers to track metrics such as losses, accuracy, gradients, and model parameters, as well as inspect data and track the progress of experiments. Integration with TensorFlow makes it easy to configure, making it indispensable for optimizing models and identifying issues during training.

Configuring TensorBoard to Monitor Metrics

Configuring TensorBoard starts with creating a directory where logs will be stored. These logs contain information about the metrics that will be viewed in the TensorBoard interface. In TensorFlow, logging is done using the callback `tf.keras.callbacks.TensorBoard`.

Environment Preparation

Before configuring TensorBoard, you must ensure that TensorFlow and TensorBoard are installed. To install TensorBoard, use:

bash

```
pip install tensorboard
```

Callback Configuration

O callback TensorBoard captures metrics during training and writes them to the specified directory. It can be added directly to the method fit model:

python

```
import tensorflow as tf
from tensorflow.keras import Sequential
from tensorflow.keras.layers import Dense

# Creating a simple model
model = Sequential([
    Dense(64, activation='relu', input_shape=(100,)),
    Dense(32, activation='relu'),
    Dense(1, activation='sigmoid')
])

# Compiling the model
model.compile(optimizer='adam', loss='binary_crossentropy',
metrics=['accuracy'])

# Creating the directory to store logs
log_dir = "./logs"

# Configuring the TensorBoard callback
tensorboard_callback =
tf.keras.callbacks.TensorBoard(log_dir=log_dir,
histogram_freq=1)

# Generating dummy data
import numpy as np
X_train = np.random.random((1000, 100))
y_train = np.random.randint(0, 2, (1000,))

# Training the model with TensorBoard
model.fit(X_train, y_train, epochs=10, batch_size=32,
callbacks=[tensorboard_callback])
```

Starting TensorBoard

After training begins, launch TensorBoard to view the logs. In the terminal, run:

bash

```
tensorboard --logdir=./logs
```

Then, access the address provided, usually http://localhost:6006, to explore the TensorBoard interface.

Monitored Metrics

TensorBoard presents different types of graphs and information:

1. **Scalars**: View metrics such as loss and accuracy across epochs.
2. **Histograms**: Shows the distribution of weights and gradients during training.
3. **Distributions**: Tracks how weights change over time.
4. **Images**: View model inputs and outputs, such as convolution filters.
5. **Model Graphics**: Inspects the model structure and data flows.

Gradient Analysis and Model Parameters

TensorBoard is also a powerful tool for inspecting gradients and model parameters. These features help you understand model behavior during training and diagnose issues like missing or exploding gradients.

Gradient Registration

To display gradients, ative or record non-callback histograms:

python

```
tensorboard_callback =
tf.keras.callbacks.TensorBoard(log_dir=log_dir,
histogram_freq=1)
```

This will allow TensorBoard to record gradient distributions at each epoch, displaying how they vary across different layers of the model.

Exploring Model Weights

Model weights can be monitored to ensure they are not becoming too large or too small, which could indicate training issues. In TensorBoard, histograms show how weight values are distributed over time.

python

```
# Viewing model weights
for layer in model.layers:
    weights = layer.get_weights()
    print(f"Layer weights {layer.name}: {weights}")
```

Inspection of Model Structures

TensorBoard also allows you to visualize the model structure. To do this, save the computational graph during training:

python

```
# Adding the model graph to TensorBoard
tensorboard_callback =
tf.keras.callbacks.TensorBoard(log_dir=log_dir,
```

```
write_graph=True)
```

In the TensorBoard interface, the "Graph" tab presents a detailed view of the model, including data flows between layers.

Data Visualization with TensorBoard

In addition to monitoring training metrics, TensorBoard can be used to visualize model inputs and outputs. For example, when training a convolutional network, you can inspect input images and the learned filters.

Image Registration

TensorBoard allows you to record images during training:

python

```
file_writer = tf.summary.create_file_writer(log_dir + "/images")

# Registering input images
with file_writer.as_default():
    tf.summary.image("Input images", X_train[:10].reshape(-1,
10, 10, 1), step=0)
```

Inspection of Filters and Activations

For convolutional networks, visualizing filters and activations can help you understand how the model is processing the data:

python

```
# Getting filters from a convolutional layer
from tensorflow.keras.models import Model

model_conv = Sequential([
    tf.keras.layers.Conv2D(32, (3, 3), activation='relu',
input_shape=(28, 28, 1)),
    tf.keras.layers.MaxPooling2D((2, 2)),
```

```
    tf.keras.layers.Flatten(),
    tf.keras.layers.Dense(10, activation='softmax')
])

# Viewing the filters
filters, biases = model_conv.layers[0].get_weights()
print(f"Layer filters: {filters.shape}")

# Creating a model to inspect activations
activation_model = Model(inputs=model_conv.input,
outputs=model_conv.layers[0].output)
activations = activation_model.predict(X_train[:1])
```

Metrics-Based Optimization

One of the biggest advantages of TensorBoard is that it allows adjustments during training based on the metrics viewed. For example, if the gradients in some layers are disappearing, techniques such as gradient normalization or learning rate adjustments can be applied.

python

```
# Changing learning rate based on performance
new_lr = 0.001
tf.keras.backend.set_value(model.optimizer.learning_rate,
new_lr)
```

TensorBoard is more than a visualization tool; it is a strategic component in the development of deep learning models. It provides in-depth training insights, helping you diagnose issues and refine models for peak performance. With its intuitive interface and integration with TensorFlow, TensorBoard is a must-have for any deep learning pipeline.

CHAPTER 16: APPLICATIONS IN IOT

The Internet of Things (IoT) is an exponentially growing field, connecting smart devices that collect, share and process data in real time. These devices range from sensors and cameras to voice assistants and industrial systems. With the popularization of IoT comes the need to process data directly on the device, an approach known as edge computing. TensorFlow Lite (TFLite) was developed to meet these demands, enabling deep learning models to run on embedded devices with limited computing resources.

Using TensorFlow Lite on Embedded Devices

TensorFlow Lite is an optimized version of TensorFlow designed to run on mobile and embedded devices. It reduces the size of models and improves their efficiency without significantly sacrificing accuracy. Additionally, TFLite is compatible with multiple hardware architectures, including CPUs, GPUs, and specialized accelerators such as TPUs and microcontrollers.

TensorFlow Lite Workflow

Using TensorFlow Lite follows a structured workflow:

1. **Model Training**
   The model is trained using TensorFlow in a conventional development environment, such as a computer or server.
2. **Conversion to TFLite**

After training, the model is converted to the TFLite format, which is lighter and optimized for embedded devices.

3. **On-Device Implementation**
   The converted model is deployed to the IoT device, where it can perform real-time inferences.
4. **Integration with Applications**
   The TFLite model is integrated into specific applications for automation, monitoring or any other desired functionality.

Model Conversion for TFLite

After training a model with TensorFlow, it can be converted to TFLite format using the converter `TFLiteConverter`. Below is the process to convert an image classification model:

python

```
import tensorflow as tf

# Training a simple model
from tensorflow.keras import Sequential
from tensorflow.keras.layers import Dense, Flatten

model = Sequential([
    Flatten(input_shape=(28, 28)),
    Dense(128, activation='relu'),
    Dense(10, activation='softmax')
])

# Compiling and training the model
model.compile(optimizer='adam',
loss='sparse_categorical_crossentropy', metrics=['accuracy'])
model.fit(X_train, y_train, epochs=5)

# Saving the model in TensorFlow format
model.save("model")

# Converting the model to TensorFlow Lite
```

```
converter = tf.lite.TFLiteConverter.from_saved_model("model")
tflite_model = converter.convert()

# Saving the TFLite model
with open("model.tflite", "wb") as f:
    f.write(tflite_model)
```

Integration into IoT Devices

Once converted, the TFLite model can be implemented on IoT devices such as Raspberry Pi, Arduino or other microcontrollers. TensorFlow Lite provides APIs for several languages, including Python, C++, and Java, to facilitate this integration.

Python implementation on Raspberry Pi

On Raspberry Pi, the model can be used to perform real-time inference:

python

```
import tensorflow as tf
import numpy as np
from PIL import Image

# Loading the TFLite model
interpreter = tf.lite.Interpreter(model_path="model.tflite")
interpreter.allocate_tensors()

# Getting details of inputs and outputs
input_details = interpreter.get_input_details()
output_details = interpreter.get_output_details()

# Loading a test image
image = Image.open("test_image.jpg").resize((28,
28)).convert('L')
input_data = np.expand_dims(np.array(image,
dtype=np.float32), axis=0)
```

```
# Performing the inference
interpreter.set_tensor(input_details[0]['index'], input_data)
interpreter.invoke()
output_data = interpreter.get_tensor(output_details[0]['index'])

print("Inference result:", output_data)
```

Practical Examples in Edge Computing

Edge computing is essential for many IoT applications as it reduces latency, saves bandwidth, and improves privacy by processing data locally. Some practical examples include:

Image Recognition

Embedded devices can use TFLite models for object recognition, such as in smart security cameras or industrial monitoring devices.

Configuring a Model for Object Recognition

The MobileNet model, optimized for mobile devices, can be used for object recognition:

python

```
from tensorflow.keras.applications import MobileNet
from tensorflow.keras.applications.mobilenet import
preprocess_input

# Loading and converting the MobileNet model
mobilenet_model = MobileNet(weights='imagenet',
include_top=True)

converter =
tf.lite.TFLiteConverter.from_keras_model(mobilenet_model)
tflite_model = converter.convert()
```

```
with open("mobilenet.tflite", "wb") as f:
    f.write(tflite_model)
```

On-Device Implementation

Once converted, the model can be used to classify objects in images captured by a camera connected to the device.

Sensor Monitoring

In industrial or home automation applications, IoT devices can use TFLite models to detect anomalies or patterns in sensor data.

Sensor Data Analysis

TensorFlow Lite can be combined with sensors connected to microcontrollers, such as Arduino, to monitor vibrations in industrial machines:

python

```
import serial
import tensorflow as tf
import numpy as np

# Configuring communication with Arduino
ser = serial.Serial('COM3', 9600)

# Loading the TFLite model
interpreter =
tf.lite.Interpreter(model_path="sensor_model.tflite")
interpreter.allocate_tensors()

input_details = interpreter.get_input_details()
output_details = interpreter.get_output_details()
```

```
while True:
    # Reading sensor data
    sensor_data = ser.readline()
    input_data = np.array([float(sensor_data)],
dtype=np.float32).reshape(1, -1)

    # Performing inference
    interpreter.set_tensor(input_details[0]['index'], input_data)
    interpreter.invoke()
    output = interpreter.get_tensor(output_details[0]['index'])

    print("Sensor analysis:", output)
```

Home Automation

In smart home systems, IoT devices can use TFLite models to interpret voice commands, detect faces, or control devices based on environmental conditions.

Voice Recognition

TensorFlow Lite also supports models for speech recognition, such as the Wake Word Detection model:

python

```
import sounddevice as sd

# Capturing audio in real time
def record_audio(duration, samplerate=16000):
    return sd.rec(int(duration * samplerate),
samplerate=samplerate, channels=1, dtype='int16')

audio_data = record_audio(3) # 3 second recording

# Performing inference
interpreter =
tf.lite.Interpreter(model_path="wake_word_model.tflite")
interpreter.allocate_tensors()
interpreter.set_tensor(input_details[0]['index'], audio_data)
interpreter.invoke()
result = interpreter.get_tensor(output_details[0]['index'])
```

```
print("Command recognized:", result)
```

TensorFlow Lite is a powerful tool for bringing deep learning to the world of IoT, enabling embedded devices to perform sophisticated inference directly at the edge. With its ability to optimize models and easily integrate them with low-power devices, it enables innovations in diverse areas, from automation to health and safety. By exploring these technologies, developers can create efficient, intelligent and highly scalable solutions for the connected future.

CHAPTER 17: DISTRIBUTED TRAINING

Training deep learning models on large datasets can be a computationally intensive task. The need to accelerate training and deal with complex models has led to the development of distributed training strategies, which use multiple GPUs, TPUs or clusters of machines to share the computational load. TensorFlow offers robust tools for configuring and managing these environments, allowing developers to scale their model training efficiently.

Distributed Training Fundamentals

Distributed training divides the training work across multiple compute units, which can be GPUs, TPUs, or machines in a cluster. There are different strategies to implement this training:

1. **Synchronized Training**
   All devices work together on each batch of data, sharing gradients to update weights consistently.
2. **Asynchronous Training**
   Each device updates weights independently based on locally calculated gradients.
3. **Hybrid Training**
   It combines aspects of synchronous and asynchronous training to take advantage of the benefits of both methods.

TensorFlow Simplifies Distributed Training Through API tf.distribute, which provides support for configuring specific strategies based on the execution environment.

Multiple GPU Configuration

GPUs are widely used in deep learning due to their ability to perform intensive mathematical operations in parallel. Using multiple GPUs for distributed training is one of the most common ways to speed up the process.

Strategy MirroredStrategy

The strategy tf.distribute.MirroredStrategy allows you to distribute training across multiple GPUs on a single machine. All devices process different batches of data in parallel and synchronize the gradients after each iteration.

python

```
import tensorflow as tf
from tensorflow.keras import Sequential
from tensorflow.keras.layers import Dense, Flatten

# Configuring the strategy for multiple GPUs
strategy = tf.distribute.MirroredStrategy()

# Creating and training the model within the scope of the
strategy
with strategy.scope():
    model = Sequential([
        Flatten(input_shape=(28, 28)),
        Dense(128, activation='relu'),
        Dense(10, activation='softmax')
    ])
    model.compile(optimizer='adam',
loss='sparse_categorical_crossentropy', metrics=['accuracy'])
```

```
# Generating dummy data
import numpy as np
X_train = np.random.random((10000, 28, 28))
y_train = np.random.randint(0, 10, (10000,))

# Training the model
model.fit(X_train, y_train, epochs=10, batch_size=64)
```

By using this strategy, TensorFlow automatically distributes batches of data across available GPUs while maintaining consistency in model weights.

Configuring Compute Clusters

Compute clusters enable large-scale training by distributing work across multiple machines, each with one or more GPUs. This approach is useful for extremely large datasets and models.

Strategy MultiWorkerMirroredStrategy

The strategy tf.distribute.MultiWorkerMirroredStrategy allows multiple machines to collaborate on training, synchronizing gradients after each iteration.

Cluster Configuration

The cluster needs to be configured with a definition that specifies the machines and their roles (for example, worker or primary server):

python

```
import json

cluster_spec = {
    "worker": ["worker1:12345", "worker2:12345"]
}
with open("cluster.json", "w") as f:
    json.dump(cluster_spec, f)
```

The environment variable TF_CONFIG is used to tell TensorFlow about the cluster:

bash

```
export TF_CONFIG='{
    "cluster": {
        "worker": ["worker1:12345", "worker2:12345"]
    },
    "task": {"type": "worker", "index": 0}
}'
```

Distributed Training

Within the Python code, training is configured with the strategy MultiWorkerMirroredStrategy:

python

```
strategy = tf.distribute.MultiWorkerMirroredStrategy()

with strategy.scope():
    model = Sequential([
        Flatten(input_shape=(28, 28)),
        Dense(128, activation='relu'),
        Dense(10, activation='softmax')
    ])
    model.compile(optimizer='adam',
loss='sparse_categorical_crossentropy', metrics=['accuracy'])

model.fit(X_train, y_train, epochs=10, batch_size=64)
```

This setup allows multiple machines to work together on model training, sharing gradients efficiently.

Training Acceleration for Large Datasets

Large datasets are challenging due to the time required to load and process them. To optimize performance, additional strategies can be applied:

Data Preprocessing with tf.data

A API tf.data is used to create efficient data pipelines, which can be integrated into distributed training.

python

```
dataset = tf.data.Dataset.from_tensor_slices((X_train, y_train))
dataset =
dataset.shuffle(buffer_size=10000).batch(64).prefetch(buffer_si
ze=tf.data.AUTOTUNE)
```

Use of TPUs

TPUs (Tensor Processing Units) are specialized accelerators for deep learning. TensorFlow makes it easier to use TPUs through the strategy TPUStrategy.

python

```
resolver =
tf.distribute.cluster_resolver.TPUClusterResolver(tpu='your_tp
u_name')
tf.config.experimental_connect_to_cluster(resolver)
tf.tpu.experimental.initialize_tpu_system(resolver)

strategy = tf.distribute.TPUStrategy(resolver)

with strategy.scope():
    model = Sequential([
        Flatten(input_shape=(28, 28)),
        Dense(128, activation='relu'),
        Dense(10, activation='softmax')
    ])
    model.compile(optimizer='adam',
loss='sparse_categorical_crossentropy', metrics=['accuracy'])
```

```
model.fit(X_train, y_train, epochs=10, batch_size=128)
```

Checkpoints for Training Recovery

Saving checkpoints during training ensures that the process can be resumed in case of failure. TensorFlow supports this:

python

```
checkpoint_path = "training_checkpoints/cp-{epoch:04d}.ckpt"

cp_callback = tf.keras.callbacks.ModelCheckpoint(
    filepath=checkpoint_path,
    save_weights_only=True,
    verbose=1
)

model.fit(X_train, y_train, epochs=10, batch_size=64,
callbacks=[cp_callback])
```

Distributed Training Monitoring

TensorBoard can be used to monitor training metrics in real time, even in distributed settings:

python

```
log_dir = "./logs"
tensorboard_callback =
tf.keras.callbacks.TensorBoard(log_dir=log_dir)

model.fit(X_train, y_train, epochs=10, batch_size=64,
callbacks=[tensorboard_callback])
```

Distributed training is a powerful tool for addressing scalability challenges in deep learning. With TensorFlow's robust support, you can configure efficient environments to use multiple GPUs,

TPUs, or entire clusters. This approach not only speeds up training, but also allows you to explore more complex models and larger datasets, opening new horizons in the development of deep learning-based solutions.

CHAPTER 18: MODEL EXPORT AND DEPLOYMENT

Model export and deployment are crucial steps in the lifecycle of a deep learning model. Once training is complete, the model needs to be made available for consumption, whether by on-premises applications or in a cloud production environment. TensorFlow offers robust tools for exporting models in supported formats and deploying them using TensorFlow Serving, APIs, or cloud services.

Export with SavedModel

The SavedModel format is TensorFlow's default for saving trained models. It preserves the architecture, weights, and information needed to continue training or perform inferences. SavedModel is highly flexible, supporting APIs from different languages, such as Python, C++ and Java.

Saving a Model

After training, a model can be saved in SavedModel format using the method `model.save()`:

python

```
import tensorflow as tf
from tensorflow.keras import Sequential
from tensorflow.keras.layers import Dense

# Creating and training a simple model
```

```
model = Sequential([
    Dense(128, activation='relu', input_shape=(100,)),
    Dense(10, activation='softmax')
])

model.compile(optimizer='adam',
loss='sparse_categorical_crossentropy', metrics=['accuracy'])

# Dummy data
import numpy as np
X_train = np.random.random((1000, 100))
y_train = np.random.randint(0, 10, size=(1000,))

model.fit(X_train, y_train, epochs=5, batch_size=32)

# Saving the model in SavedModel format
model.save("saved_model/my_model")
```

The directory `saved_model/my_model` will contain the saved model, including weights, architecture and metadata.

Loading a SavedModel Model

A saved model can be loaded to continue training or perform inferences:

python

```
# Loading the saved model
loaded_model = tf.keras.models.load_model("saved_model/
my_model")

# Performing inferences with the loaded model
predictions = loaded_model.predict(X_train[:10])
print(predictions)
```

Conversion to Other Formats

TensorFlow Lite and TensorFlow.js enable models to be used

on mobile, embedded devices, and web browsers. To convert a model to TensorFlow Lite:

python

```
converter =
tf.lite.TFLiteConverter.from_saved_model("saved_model/
my_model")
tflite_model = converter.convert()

# Saving the model in TFLite format
with open("model.tflite", "wb") as f:
    f.write(tflite_model)
```

To export to TensorFlow.js:

bash

```
pip install tensorflowjs
tensorflowjs_converter --input_format=tf_saved_model --
output_node_names='dense_1' --saved_model_tags=serve ./
saved_model/my_model ./tfjs_model
```

Deploy Using TensorFlow Serving

TensorFlow Serving is a deployment platform that provides a REST API for serving trained models. It is optimized for high performance and scalability, making it ideal for production.

TensorFlow Serving Configuration

To use TensorFlow Serving, you need to install it. On Linux-based systems, installation can be done via Docker:

bash

```
docker pull tensorflow/serving
```

Serving a Model

To serve a saved model, start TensorFlow Serving by specifying the model path:

bash

```
docker run -p 8501:8501 --name=tf_serving --mount type=bind,source=$(pwd)/saved_model/my_model,target=/models/my_model -e MODEL_NAME=my_model -t tensorflow/serving
```

The model will be available in the REST API at http://localhost:8501/v1/models/my_model:predict.

Performing Inferences with TensorFlow Serving

After the model is being served, use tools like curl or Python libraries to send inference requests:

python

```
import requests
import numpy as np

# Input data for inference
data = {
    "instances": np.random.random((1, 100)).tolist()
}

# Request to the REST API
response = requests.post("http://localhost:8501/v1/models/my_model:predict", json=data)
print("Inference result:", response.json())
```

Deploy in the Cloud

In addition to TensorFlow Serving, cloud services offer complete solutions for model deployment. Platforms like Google Cloud AI Platform, AWS SageMaker, and Azure Machine Learning simplify the process of scaling models to millions of users.

Deploy no Google Cloud AI Platform

Google Cloud AI Platform allows you to import models directly in SavedModel format and expose them as REST APIs.

Prepare the Environment
Make sure you have the Google Cloud SDK installed and authenticated:

bash

```
gcloud auth login
```

Upload the Template
Upload the model to your Google Cloud Storage bucket:

bash

```
gsutil cp -r saved_model/my_model gs://your-bucket-name/
my_model
```

Create an Endpoint
Register the model on AI Platform:

bash

```
gcloud ai models upload --region=us-central1 --display-
name=my_model --artifact-uri=gs://your-bucket-name/
my_model
```

Serve the Model

Create an endpoint for the model:

bash

```
gcloud ai endpoints create --region=us-central1 --display-name=my_endpoint
```

Make Inferences
Send data to the created endpoint:

python

```
from google.cloud import aiplatform

endpoint = aiplatform.Endpoint("projects/your-project-id/locations/us-central1/endpoints/your-endpoint-id")
response = endpoint.predict([{"input_data": np.random.random((100,)).tolist()}])
print("Inference result:", response.predictions)
```

Deploy to Other Clouds

Other platforms such as AWS SageMaker and Azure Machine Learning also offer support for TensorFlow and direct integration with deployment and scalability tools.

Model Monitoring and Update

After deployment, it is important to monitor the model's performance and update it as necessary. Some practices include:

- **Continuous Monitoring**: Use tools like Google Cloud Monitoring to track usage and performance metrics.
- **Model Update**: Reimport new models to existing endpoints for non-disruptive updates.
- **Versioning**: Save model versions to track changes and allow reprocessing with old models.

Exporting and deploying models is a crucial step in transforming deep learning models into practical and scalable solutions. With the support of TensorFlow and tools like TensorFlow Serving and cloud services, developers can deploy models in production environments, ensuring high availability and performance. TensorFlow's flexibility to integrate with multiple platforms makes it a robust choice for large-scale deployment.

CHAPTER 19: OPTIMIZERS AND LOSS FUNCTIONS

Optimizers and loss functions are essential components in training neural networks. Together, they determine how the model adjusts its weights to minimize error and achieve better results. The correct choice of an optimizer and loss function can significantly impact model performance, influencing convergence speed, accuracy and training stability.

Analysis of Top Optimizers

Optimizers adjust the weights of neural networks based on gradients calculated during training. They implement different strategies to determine how these adjustments are made. Among the most used optimizers are SGD, Adam and RMSprop.

Stochastic Gradient Descent (SGD)

SGD is one of the most basic and widely used optimizers. It adjusts the weights iteratively, based on small subsets of the dataset, called minibatches. This reduces the computational cost per iteration compared to calculating the gradient on the entire dataset.

python

```
import tensorflow as tf

# Configuring the SGD optimizer
optimizer = tf.keras.optimizers.SGD(learning_rate=0.01,
```

```
momentum=0.9)
```

The use of momentum in SGD allows it to consider previous gradients, helping to overcome local minima and speeding up convergence.

Adam (Adaptive Moment Estimation)

Adam combines the benefits of RMSprop and SGD with momentum. It adjusts the learning rate of each weight individually based on accumulated gradients and their variances. This results in more efficient training, especially for deep networks and noisy data.

python

```
# Configuring the Adam optimizer
optimizer = tf.keras.optimizers.Adam(learning_rate=0.001)
```

Adam is often the default choice because of its robustness and ability to handle different types of learning problems.

RMSprop

RMSprop dynamically adapts the learning rate based on the magnitude of recent gradients. It is widely used in recurrent networks such as LSTMs and GRUs due to its ability to handle oscillating gradients well.

python

```
# Configuring the RMSprop optimizer
optimizer = tf.keras.optimizers.RMSprop(learning_rate=0.001)
```

RMSprop is effective on problems with gradients that vary widely in magnitude.

Comparison and Choice of Optimizers

The choice of optimizer depends on the specific problem and data behavior:

- **SGD** It is ideal for smaller problems and when simplicity is required.
- **Adam** It is highly versatile and works well for most tasks.
- **RMSprop** is a good choice for problems involving highly oscillating sequences or gradients.

Choosing Loss Functions for Different Tasks

Loss functions calculate the error between model predictions and actual values. They guide training by adjusting weights to minimize error. Each type of problem requires an appropriate loss function.

Regression

Regression problems predict continuous values. The most common loss functions include:

1. **Mean Squared Error (MSE)**
   Calculates the mean of the squared errors. It penalizes large errors more severely, making it suitable for problems where large deviations are undesirable.

python

```
# Configuring the MSE loss function
loss = tf.keras.losses.MeanSquaredError()
```

2. **Mean Absolute Error (MAE)**
   Calculates the average of absolute errors, being more robust against outliers than MSE.

python

```
# Configuring the MAE loss function
loss = tf.keras.losses.MeanAbsoluteError()
```

Classification

Classification problems categorize inputs into distinct classes. The most commonly used loss functions include:

1. **Sparse Categorical Crossentropy**
   Suitable for multiclass classification problems with integer labels.

python

```
# Configuring the Sparse Categorical Crossentropy loss function
loss = tf.keras.losses.SparseCategoricalCrossentropy()
```

2. **Categorical Crossentropy**
   Used when labels are in one-hot encoding format.

python

```
# Configuring the Categorical Crossentropy loss function
loss = tf.keras.losses.CategoricalCrossentropy()
```

3. **Binary Crossentropy**
   Used for binary classification problems.

python

```
# Configuring the Binary Crossentropy loss function
loss = tf.keras.losses.BinaryCrossentropy()
```

Anomaly Detection

Anomaly detection problems, such as autoencoders, require custom loss functions to measure reconstruction of the inputs.

python

```
# Custom loss function for autoencoders
def custom_loss(y_true, y_pred):
    return tf.reduce_mean(tf.square(y_true - y_pred))
```

Generative Networks and Advanced Tasks

Generative models, like GANs, use specialized loss functions for the generators and discriminators:

python

```
# Loss function for the discriminator
discriminator_loss = tf.keras.losses.BinaryCrossentropy()

# Loss function for the generator
generator_loss = tf.keras.losses.BinaryCrossentropy()
```

Configuring the Optimizer and Loss Function in the Model

Optimizers and loss functions are configured in the method `compile` from the Keras model:

python

```
model.compile(optimizer='adam',
loss='sparse_categorical_crossentropy', metrics=['accuracy'])
```

Adjustment and Monitoring During Training

Tuning hyperparameters like learning rate is essential to achieve the best results. Callbacks, like `LearningRateScheduler`, allow dynamic adjustments:

python

```
# Adjusting the learning rate dynamically
def scheduler(epoch, lr):
    if epoch < 10:
        return lr
    else:
        return lr * tf.math.exp(-0.1)

lr_callback =
tf.keras.callbacks.LearningRateScheduler(scheduler)
model.fit(X_train, y_train, epochs=20, callbacks=[lr_callback])
```

Monitoring with TensorBoard

TensorBoard can be used to visualize metrics related to the optimizer and loss function during training:

python

```
log_dir = "./logs"
tensorboard_callback =
tf.keras.callbacks.TensorBoard(log_dir=log_dir)

model.fit(X_train, y_train, epochs=10,
callbacks=[tensorboard_callback])
```

Optimizers and loss functions are cornerstones in training neural networks. Understanding its characteristics and choosing the most appropriate options for each problem is essential to achieving optimal performance. The combination of robust optimizers, appropriate loss functions, and effective tuning strategies ensures more accurate and efficient models, ready to solve the most complex challenges in deep learning.

CHAPTER 20: BENCHMARKING AND OPTIMIZATION

Efficient performance is essential in deep learning projects, especially when working with large datasets and complex models. Identifying performance bottlenecks and applying practical optimizations can reduce training time, improve inference capability, and optimize the use of computing resources. This chapter covers benchmarking techniques and optimization strategies to achieve maximum efficiency.

Identification of Performance Bottlenecks

Before implementing any optimization, it is critical to understand where the model's performance is being limited. The main bottlenecks can be categorized into three areas: compute, memory, and input/output.

Benchmarking no TensorFlow

TensorFlow provides tools to monitor training performance and identify potential bottlenecks. The API tf.profiler is a robust solution for capturing detailed information about resource usage during training.

Uso do Profiler

Profiler allows you to track model execution and generate detailed reports. It can be activated directly in code:

python

```
import tensorflow as tf

# Configuring the Profiler
log_dir = "./logs"
tf.profiler.experimental.start(log_dir)

# Training the model
model = tf.keras.Sequential([
    tf.keras.layers.Dense(128, activation='relu',
input_shape=(100,)),
    tf.keras.layers.Dense(10, activation='softmax')
])
model.compile(optimizer='adam',
loss='sparse_categorical_crossentropy', metrics=['accuracy'])

X_train = tf.random.normal((1000, 100))
y_train = tf.random.uniform((1000,), minval=0, maxval=10,
dtype=tf.int32)

model.fit(X_train, y_train, epochs=5, batch_size=32)

# Finishing the Profiler
tf.profiler.experimental.stop()
```

Once configured, the report can be viewed in TensorBoard, identifying where the model spends the most time.

Monitoring Essential Metrics

Monitoring metrics like CPU, GPU, memory, and I/O time usage helps you identify specific bottlenecks:

- **Uso and GPU**: Monitor GPU usage with tools like nvidia-smi.
- **I/O Latency**: Identify if data loading is a bottleneck using the pipeline tf.data com prefetch.
- **Memory**: Monitor memory consumption to avoid overflows and optimize allocations.

Practical Optimizations for Greater Computational Efficiency

After identifying the bottlenecks, it is time to implement optimizations that increase computational efficiency. Strategies range from hyperparameter tuning to revamping the training pipeline.

Data Pipeline Optimization

An efficient data pipeline is crucial to prevent data loading from becoming a bottleneck.

Use of tf.data for Data Manipulation

A API tf.data is designed to build optimized pipelines that can be used directly in model training.

python

```
dataset = tf.data.Dataset.from_tensor_slices((X_train, y_train))
dataset =
dataset.shuffle(buffer_size=10000).batch(32).prefetch(buffer_si
ze=tf.data.AUTOTUNE)
```

The method prefetch allows data to be loaded in parallel with model execution, reducing idle time.

Caching

For datasets that fit in memory, the method cache can be used to avoid repeated reads from the disk:

python

```
dataset =
dataset.cache().prefetch(buffer_size=tf.data.AUTOTUNE)
```

Uso de Mixed Precision

Mixed Precision training uses 16-bit floating point numbers (float16) instead of 32-bit (float32), reducing memory usage and speeding up calculations. In TensorFlow this can be enabled with tf.keras.mixed_precision.

python

```
from tensorflow.keras.mixed_precision import
set_global_policy

# Configuring the use of mixed precision
set_global_policy('mixed_float16')

# Creating a model with mixed precision
model = tf.keras.Sequential([
    tf.keras.layers.Dense(128, activation='relu',
input_shape=(100,)),
    tf.keras.layers.Dense(10, activation='softmax')
])
model.compile(optimizer='adam',
loss='sparse_categorical_crossentropy', metrics=['accuracy'])
```

Use of Parallelism

Parallelism can be applied at various stages of training to speed up processing.

Distributed Training with Multiple GPUs

Using multiple GPUs allows you to divide the work, increasing efficiency:

python

```
strategy = tf.distribute.MirroredStrategy()
```

```
with strategy.scope():
    model = tf.keras.Sequential([
        tf.keras.layers.Dense(128, activation='relu',
input_shape=(100,)),
        tf.keras.layers.Dense(10, activation='softmax')
    ])
    model.compile(optimizer='adam',
loss='sparse_categorical_crossentropy', metrics=['accuracy'])
```

Parallelism in the Data Pipeline

The method map can be used to apply transformations in parallel in the data pipeline:

python

```
dataset = dataset.map(lambda x, y: (x / 255.0, y),
num_parallel_calls=tf.data.AUTOTUNE)
```

Model Optimization

Models can be optimized to reduce complexity without significantly sacrificing accuracy.

Regularization and Dropout

Regularization prevents overfitting, while Dropout reduces model complexity:

python

```
from tensorflow.keras.layers import Dropout

model = tf.keras.Sequential([
    tf.keras.layers.Dense(128, activation='relu',
input_shape=(100,)),
```

```
    tf.keras.layers.Dropout(0.5),
    tf.keras.layers.Dense(10, activation='softmax')
])
```

Quantization

Quantization reduces the precision of weights to optimize models for resource-limited devices:

python

```
converter =
tf.lite.TFLiteConverter.from_saved_model("saved_model/
my_model")
converter.optimizations = [tf.lite.Optimize.DEFAULT]
tflite_model = converter.convert()

with open("quantized_model.tflite", "wb") as f:
    f.write(tflite_model)
```

Continuous Monitoring and Refinement

Continuously monitoring performance and adjusting optimizations as needed is essential to maintaining efficiency.

Callback to Adjust Learning Rate

Callbacks can dynamically adjust the learning rate:

python

```
lr_scheduler =
tf.keras.callbacks.LearningRateScheduler(lambda epoch: 1e-3 *
10**(-epoch / 20))
model.fit(X_train, y_train, epochs=10, callbacks=[lr_scheduler])
```

TensorBoard for Performance Analysis

TensorBoard helps you visualize performance metrics and identify bottlenecks:

python

```
tensorboard_callback =
tf.keras.callbacks.TensorBoard(log_dir="./logs")
model.fit(X_train, y_train, epochs=10,
callbacks=[tensorboard_callback])
```

Benchmarking and optimization are continuous processes that ensure deep learning models are trained and run efficiently. By identifying bottlenecks and applying practical strategies, it is possible to reduce computational costs, accelerate training and implement more scalable solutions. Leveraging TensorFlow tools and techniques to monitor, optimize, and refine models is an essential skill for any developer or data scientist who wants to maximize the potential of their solutions.

CHAPTER 21: SECURITY AND ROBUSTNESS IN MODELS

As deep learning models become more widely used in critical applications such as healthcare, finance, and public safety, ensuring their robustness and protection against adversarial attacks is a priority. This chapter covers techniques to prevent attacks, test the robustness of models, and implement strategies to increase their reliability in real-world scenarios.

Preventing Adversary Attacks

Deep learning models are vulnerable to adversarial attacks, where small perturbations in input data can lead to incorrect or unexpected results. These attacks can be divided into categories such as avoidance (evasion) attacks, extraction attacks, and poison attacks.

Avoidance Attacks

Avoidance attacks are designed to trick the model during inference. For example, an image can be modified in a way that is imperceptible to humans, but which results in incorrect classifications by the model.

Generating Adversarial Examples

In TensorFlow, adversarial examples can be generated using input gradients to create computed perturbations:

python

```
import tensorflow as tf

# Loading a trained model
model = tf.keras.models.load_model("saved_model/my_model")

# Defining a function to generate adversarial examples
def create_adversarial_example(model, input_image,
target_label, epsilon=0.1):
    input_image = tf.convert_to_tensor(input_image)
    target_label = tf.convert_to_tensor(target_label)

    with tf.GradientTape() as tape:
        tape.watch(input_image)
        prediction = model(input_image)
        loss = tf.keras.losses.SparseCategoricalCrossentropy()
(target_label, prediction)

    gradient = tape.gradient(loss, input_image)
    adversarial_image = input_image + epsilon * tf.sign(gradient)
    return tf.clip_by_value(adversarial_image, 0, 1)

# Generating an adversarial image
adversarial_image = create_adversarial_example(model,
input_image, target_label)
```

Avoidance Attack Prevention

Measures to protect models against avoidance attacks include:

1. **Adversary Training**
   Add adversarial examples to training to improve model robustness:

python

```
# Creating a data pipeline with adversarial examples
def adversarial_training_data(dataset, model):
    augmented_data = []
    for image, label in dataset:
        adversarial_image = create_adversarial_example(model,
```

```
image, label)
        augmented_data.append((adversarial_image, label))
    return tf.data.Dataset.from_tensor_slices(augmented_data)
```

2. **Gradient Regularization**
   Increase the penalty on large gradients to reduce sensitivity to small changes:

python

```
def gradient_regularization_loss(y_true, y_pred, gradients,
lambda_reg=0.01):
    base_loss = tf.keras.losses.SparseCategoricalCrossentropy()
(y_true, y_pred)
    grad_loss = lambda_reg *
tf.reduce_mean(tf.square(gradients))
    return base_loss + grad_loss
```

Extraction Attacks

Extraction attacks occur when an attacker attempts to replicate model behavior without direct access to the training data. To mitigate this risk:

- **Limit Access to Inferences**: Reduce the granularity of predictions by returning only labels instead of probabilities.
- **Request Monitoring**: Implement limits on the number of requests allowed from a client or IP.

Poisoning Attacks

Poisoning attacks manipulate training data to influence model results. Prevention includes:

- **Training Data Verification**: Perform integrity checks on data before using it for training.
- **Differentially Private Training**: Apply techniques that limit the impact of a single data point on model weights.

Robustness Tests

Testing the robustness of models is essential to ensure their performance in critical scenarios. Testing includes exposing the model to unexpected inputs, such as noisy, imbalanced, or out-of-distribution data.

Testing with Noisy Data

Add noise to the inputs to check model stability:

python

```
def add_noise_to_data(data, noise_factor=0.1):
    noise = noise_factor *
tf.random.normal(shape=tf.shape(data))
    return tf.clip_by_value(data + noise, 0, 1)

# Testing the model with noisy data
noisy_data = add_noise_to_data(X_test)
predictions = model.predict(noisy_data)
```

Testing with Out-of-Distribution Data

Out-of-distribution data is input that was not represented in training. Testing with this data evaluates the model's ability to handle unexpected inputs.

python

```
# Generating data outside the distribution
ood_data = tf.random.uniform((100, 28, 28, 1), minval=0,
```

```
maxval=1)

# Performing inferences with the model
ood_predictions = model.predict(ood_data)
```

Robustness Metrics

Use metrics such as adversarial accuracy and mean confidence on out-of-distribution data to assess robustness.

Increasing Model Reliability in Critical Scenarios

Reliability is especially important in applications where errors can have serious consequences, such as health or safety.

Anomaly Detection

Add an anomaly detection system to identify inputs that the model may not be able to classify correctly:

python

```
def detect_anomalies(predictions, threshold=0.7):
    confidences = tf.reduce_max(predictions, axis=1)
    return tf.where(confidences < threshold)
```

Implementation of Committee Models

Committee models combine predictions from multiple models to increase reliability:

python

```
models = [model1, model2, model3]
```

```
def ensemble_prediction(models, input_data):
    predictions = [m.predict(input_data) for m in models]
    return tf.reduce_mean(predictions, axis=0)
```

Real-Time Monitoring

Deploy monitoring systems to capture and analyze model performance in real time:

python

```
import time

def monitor_predictions(model, stream_data):
    for data in stream_data:
        start_time = time.time()
        prediction = model.predict(data)
        latency = time.time() - start_time
        print(f"Prediction: {prediction}, Latency: {latency}")
```

Ensuring the security and robustness of deep learning models is a fundamental task in critical applications. Preventing adversarial attacks, testing the model's resilience to unexpected inputs, and implementing practices to increase its reliability are essential steps to creating secure and reliable solutions. As models become more integrated into everyday life, their protection against threats and their stability in critical scenarios become indispensable priorities.

CHAPTER 22: CASE STUDIES

Deep learning has evolved significantly, with practical applications in several areas. This chapter presents real-world case studies that demonstrate how TensorFlow can be used to solve complex problems in data classification, natural language processing (NLP), and computer vision. These examples are designed to provide a practical understanding of TensorFlow's capabilities and how to integrate it into real-world projects.

Application 1: Health Data Classification

Classifying health data is crucial in medical diagnosis, such as detecting diseases based on vital signs or laboratory tests. Here, we implement a solution to classify patients into categories based on a set of health characteristics.

Dataset Configuration

A fictitious health dataset is loaded and processed for training:

python

```
import tensorflow as tf
import numpy as np
from sklearn.model_selection import train_test_split

# Generating dummy data
np.random.seed(42)
X = np.random.rand(1000, 10) # 10 characteristics
y = np.random.randint(0, 2, 1000) # Binary labels (0 or 1)
```

```
# Splitting the dataset into training and testing
X_train, X_test, y_train, y_test = train_test_split(X, y,
test_size=0.2, random_state=42)
```

Model Construction

A simple neural network model is used for classification:

python

```
model = tf.keras.Sequential([
    tf.keras.layers.Dense(64, activation='relu',
input_shape=(10,)),
    tf.keras.layers.Dropout(0.3),
    tf.keras.layers.Dense(32, activation='relu'),
    tf.keras.layers.Dense(1, activation='sigmoid') # Binary output
])

model.compile(optimizer='adam', loss='binary_crossentropy',
metrics=['accuracy'])
```

Training and Assessment

The model is trained with the processed dataset:

python

```
model.fit(X_train, y_train, epochs=20, batch_size=32,
validation_data=(X_test, y_test))

# Evaluation on the test dataset
test_loss, test_accuracy = model.evaluate(X_test, y_test)
print(f"Test accuracy: {test_accuracy}")
```

Application 2: Natural Language Processing (NLP)

In this case study, we implemented a model for sentiment

analysis using a dataset of short texts. This task is widely applied in social media analytics and customer feedback.

Dataset Configuration

TensorFlow offers tools to easily load and process text:

python

```
from tensorflow.keras.preprocessing.text import Tokenizer
from tensorflow.keras.preprocessing.sequence import
pad_sequences

# Dummy comment data and its labels
texts = ["The service was great", "I am very disappointed",
"Amazing experience", "Not worth the money"]
labels = [1, 0, 1, 0] #1 for positive, 0 for negative

# Tokenizing texts
tokenizer = Tokenizer(num_words=1000)
tokenizer.fit_on_texts(texts)
sequences = tokenizer.texts_to_sequences(texts)

# Padding sequences to the same length
X = pad_sequences(sequences, maxlen=10)
y = np.array(labels)
```

Model Construction

An LSTM model is used to capture sequential dependencies in text:

python

```
model = tf.keras.Sequential([
    tf.keras.layers.Embedding(input_dim=1000,
output_dim=64, input_length=10),
    tf.keras.layers.LSTM(64, return_sequences=True),
    tf.keras.layers.LSTM(32),
```

```
    tf.keras.layers.Dense(1, activation='sigmoid') # Binary output
])

model.compile(optimizer='adam', loss='binary_crossentropy',
metrics=['accuracy'])
```

Training and Inference

After training, the model is used to classify new texts:

python

```
model.fit(X, y, epochs=10, batch_size=2)

# Inference in new texts
new_texts = ["The product is amazing", "Terrible experience"]
new_sequences = tokenizer.texts_to_sequences(new_texts)
new_data = pad_sequences(new_sequences, maxlen=10)

predictions = model.predict(new_data)
print("Predictions:", predictions)
```

Application 3: Computer Vision

Computer vision is widely used in tasks such as image classification, object detection and semantic segmentation. In this case study, we implemented an image classifier using the MNIST dataset.

Dataset Configuration

The MNIST dataset is loaded and preprocessed:

python

```
from tensorflow.keras.datasets import mnist

# Loading the dataset
(X_train, y_train), (X_test, y_test) = mnist.load_data()
```

```
# Normalizing the images
X_train = X_train / 255.0
X_test = X_test / 255.0

# Expanding dimensions to support convolutions
X_train = X_train[..., np.newaxis]
X_test = X_test[..., np.newaxis]
```

Model Construction

A convolutional neural network (CNN) model is used to classify the digits:

python

```
model = tf.keras.Sequential([
    tf.keras.layers.Conv2D(32, (3, 3), activation='relu',
input_shape=(28, 28, 1)),
    tf.keras.layers.MaxPooling2D((2, 2)),
    tf.keras.layers.Conv2D(64, (3, 3), activation='relu'),
    tf.keras.layers.MaxPooling2D((2, 2)),
    tf.keras.layers.Flatten(),
    tf.keras.layers.Dense(128, activation='relu'),
    tf.keras.layers.Dense(10, activation='softmax') # 10 classes
for the digits
])

model.compile(optimizer='adam',
loss='sparse_categorical_crossentropy', metrics=['accuracy'])
```

Training and Assessment

The model is trained with the MNIST dataset:

python

```
model.fit(X_train, y_train, epochs=10, batch_size=64,
validation_data=(X_test, y_test))
```

```
# Evaluation on the test dataset
test_loss, test_accuracy = model.evaluate(X_test, y_test)
print(f"Test accuracy: {test_accuracy}")
```

Real-Time Implementation

For practical demonstration, the model can be used in real-time handwritten digit recognition applications, such as on tablets or IoT devices.

Conclusion of Case Studies

These case studies show the versatility of TensorFlow in solving real-world problems in different domains. Whether it's healthcare data classification, sentiment analysis, or computer vision, TensorFlow provides the tools you need to implement robust, scalable solutions. By mastering these techniques, you will be prepared to face complex challenges and create impactful real-world applications.

CHAPTER 23: TENSORFLOW AND THE FUTURE OF AI

TensorFlow continues to be one of the most influential tools in advancing artificial intelligence (AI), shaping the future of machine learning with its ability to innovate across multiple domains. As AI expands to new horizons such as quantum computing, federated learning, and generative AI, TensorFlow evolves to meet the demands of these emerging areas. This chapter explores the latest trends in AI development, highlighting how TensorFlow is poised to play a central role in the future.

Emerging Trends in TensorFlow

TensorFlow is at the forefront of technology trends that promise to transform AI in the coming years. Some of these trends include greater accessibility to AI, integration with emerging technologies, and improving models for greater efficiency and scalability.

Democratization of AI

With the release of libraries like TensorFlow Lite and TensorFlow.js, AI has become accessible to developers on mobile devices and browsers. This enables AI-based solutions to reach a broader user base, fueling innovations in mobile apps, IoT devices, and web experiences.

Uso do TensorFlow Lite

TensorFlow Lite allows you to run optimized models on resource-constrained devices. Applications such as voice recognition on smartphones and image analysis on edge devices already benefit from this technology:

python

```
import tensorflow as tf

# Converting a model to TensorFlow Lite
converter =
tf.lite.TFLiteConverter.from_saved_model("saved_model/
my_model")
tflite_model = converter.convert()

# Saving the model
with open("model.tflite", "wb") as f:
    f.write(tflite_model)

# Inference with TensorFlow Lite
interpreter = tf.lite.Interpreter(model_path="model.tflite")
interpreter.allocate_tensors()

input_details = interpreter.get_input_details()
output_details = interpreter.get_output_details()

# Predicting with input data
interpreter.set_tensor(input_details[0]['index'], data)
interpreter.invoke()
output_data = interpreter.get_tensor(output_details[0]['index'])
```

AI on Web Devices

TensorFlow.js allows models to run directly in browsers, further democratizing access to AI. This is particularly useful in interactive applications such as games, educational tools and AI-based interfaces.

javascript

```
// Loading a model into TensorFlow.js
const model = await tf.loadLayersModel('https://example.com/
model.json');

// Making predictions
const inputTensor = tf.tensor([data]);
const prediction = model.predict(inputTensor);
prediction.print();
```

Advances in Federated Learning and Privacy

As privacy concerns rise, federated learning has gained prominence. This approach allows models to be trained directly on users' devices, without data needing to be sent to central servers.

Federated Training with TensorFlow Federated (TFF)

TensorFlow Federated is an extension that facilitates model training in distributed scenarios while preserving data privacy.

python

```
import tensorflow_federated as tff

# Configuring a federated model
def create_keras_model():
    return tf.keras.Sequential([
        tf.keras.layers.Dense(10, activation='softmax',
input_shape=(784,))
    ])

# Defining the federated task
federated_data =
[tff.simulation.FromTensorSlicesClientData(data) for data in
local_datasets]
trainer =
tff.learning.build_federated_averaging_process(create_keras_m
```

```
odel)
state = trainer.initialize()

# Training the federated model
for round_num in range(1, 11):
    state, metrics = trainer.next(state, federated_data)
    print(f"Round {round_num}, metrics={metrics}")
```

Generative AI and Fundamental Models

Generative AI and foundational models like GPT and BERT are a cornerstone of automated content creation, from text to images to music. TensorFlow continues to be a powerful platform for training and deploying these advanced models.

Training Generative Models with TensorFlow

With TensorFlow, you can implement generative adversarial networks (GANs) to create images or train models like GPT for text generation.

python

```
# Creating a GAN for image generation
generator = tf.keras.Sequential([
    tf.keras.layers.Dense(256, activation='relu',
input_shape=(100,)),
    tf.keras.layers.Reshape((16, 16, 1)),
    tf.keras.layers.Conv2DTranspose(128, (3, 3),
activation='relu', strides=(2, 2), padding='same'),
    tf.keras.layers.Conv2DTranspose(1, (3, 3), activation='tanh',
strides=(2, 2), padding='same')
])

discriminator = tf.keras.Sequential([
    tf.keras.layers.Conv2D(64, (3, 3), activation='relu',
input_shape=(64, 64, 1)),
```

```
    tf.keras.layers.Flatten(),
    tf.keras.layers.Dense(1, activation='sigmoid')
])

generator.compile(optimizer='adam',
loss='binary_crossentropy')
discriminator.compile(optimizer='adam',
loss='binary_crossentropy')
```

Quantum Computing and TensorFlow Quantum

Quantum computing is another emerging area where TensorFlow plays an essential role. With TensorFlow Quantum, researchers can integrate deep learning with quantum circuits.

Creating Quantum Circuits with TensorFlow Quantum

TensorFlow Quantum allows you to simulate and train hybrid models that combine classical and quantum computing.

python

```
import tensorflow_quantum as tfq
import cirq

# Creating a quantum circuit
qubits = [cirq.GridQubit(0, 0)]
circuit = cirq.Circuit(cirq.X(qubits[0]) ** 0.5)

# Converting the circuit to TensorFlow
quantum_data = tfq.convert_to_tensor([circuit])
```

The Role of TensorFlow in Emerging Areas

TensorFlow is shaping the future of AI by exploring emerging areas like:

- **Health and Biotechnology**: Disease prediction and drug discovery.
- **Automation and Robotics**: Control of autonomous systems in real time.
- **Sustainability**: Environmental data analysis for climate change and conservation.

The future of AI is full of possibilities, and TensorFlow continues to be a central platform for exploring these new horizons. With advances in quantum computing, federated learning, and generative AI, TensorFlow offers powerful tools for developing next-generation solutions. Being prepared for these innovations ensures that professionals in the field can make the most of the transformative potential of artificial intelligence.

CHAPTER 24: LARGE-SCALE APPLICATIONS

TensorFlow has established itself as one of the most powerful tools for deep learning, being widely adopted by companies to solve complex challenges on a large scale. From recommendation systems to financial forecasting and image analysis, TensorFlow offers solutions that can be effectively integrated into enterprise systems. This chapter addresses integration strategies in business systems, highlighting success stories that demonstrate their impact on the market.

Strategies for Integrating TensorFlow into Enterprise Systems

Integrating TensorFlow into enterprise systems requires a structured approach that ensures scalability, security, and efficiency. Below are essential strategies for successful implementation.

Systems Architecture for TensorFlow

Companies often use distributed architectures to process large volumes of data and perform real-time inferences. The typical architecture includes the following components:

1. **Data Pipeline**
   The data pipeline provides real-time or batch information to TensorFlow models. Tools like Apache Kafka or Apache Beam can be integrated for stream

processing.

2. **Models in Production**
   Models are trained and optimized in development environments and then exported to production, where they are deployed with TensorFlow Serving or cloud platforms.
3. **Cloud Infrastructure**
   TensorFlow is widely supported by cloud providers such as Google Cloud Platform (GCP), AWS, and Azure, which offer high-performance services for training and inference.

Building Data Pipelines with TensorFlow

TensorFlow offers built-in tools for creating robust pipelines, such as tf.data, which facilitates large-scale data manipulation.

python

```
import tensorflow as tf

# Loading data from a corporate source
def load_data_from_database():
    # Simulation of data received from a corporate bank
    return tf.data.Dataset.from_tensor_slices((X, y))

dataset = load_data_from_database()
dataset =
dataset.shuffle(10000).batch(64).prefetch(tf.data.AUTOTUNE)
```

Additionally, TensorFlow Extended (TFX) is a powerful framework for building end-to-end deep learning pipelines, from preprocessing to metrics analysis.

Distributed Training in Clusters

To train large-scale models, companies often use clusters with multiple GPUs or TPUs. TensorFlow simplifies this approach with distributed training strategies.

python

```
strategy = tf.distribute.MultiWorkerMirroredStrategy()

with strategy.scope():
    model = tf.keras.Sequential([
        tf.keras.layers.Dense(128, activation='relu',
input_shape=(100,)),
        tf.keras.layers.Dense(10, activation='softmax')
    ])
    model.compile(optimizer='adam',
loss='sparse_categorical_crossentropy', metrics=['accuracy'])

model.fit(dataset, epochs=10)
```

Deploy com TensorFlow Serving

After training, models are exported and served in production using TensorFlow Serving, which provides scalable REST APIs.

bash

```
docker run -p 8501:8501 --name=tf_serving --mount
type=bind,source=$(pwd)/saved_model,target=/models/
my_model -e MODEL_NAME=my_model -t tensorflow/serving
```

With the model in production, customers can send inference requests in real time:

python

```
import requests

data = {"instances": [[1.0, 2.0, 3.0]]}
response = requests.post("http://localhost:8501/v1/models/
my_model:predict", json=data)
```

```
print(response.json())
```

Success Stories in Using TensorFlow

Companies across industries have adopted TensorFlow to solve large-scale challenges. Below are three success stories that illustrate the impact of TensorFlow.

Content Recommendation System

A major streaming platform implemented TensorFlow to personalize movie and series recommendations. Using user behavior data, such as viewing history, interactions and ratings, the system is able to predict content that the user would likely watch.

Recommendation Pipeline

User data is pre-processed to feed a deep learning model such as Neural Collaborative Filtering (NCF).

python

```
import tensorflow_recommenders as tfrs

class RecommenderModel(tfrs.models.Model):
    def __init__(self):
        super().__init__()
        self.query_model = tf.keras.Sequential([
            tf.keras.layers.StringLookup(vocabulary=unique_user_
ids, mask_token=None),
            tf.keras.layers.Embedding(len(unique_user_ids) + 1,
32),
        ])
        self.candidate_model = tf.keras.Sequential([
            tf.keras.layers.StringLookup(vocabulary=unique_movi
e_titles, mask_token=None),
            tf.keras.layers.Embedding(len(unique_movie_titles) +
```

```
1, 32),
        ])
        self.task =
tfrs.tasks.Retrieval(metrics=tfrs.metrics.FactorizedTopK(candi
dates=movies.batch(128)))

    def compute_loss(self, features, training=False):
        query_embeddings =
self.query_model(features["user_id"])
        candidate_embeddings =
self.candidate_model(features["movie_title"])
        return self.task(query_embeddings,
candidate_embeddings)

model = RecommenderModel()
```

The resulting model is capable of providing real-time recommendations with high accuracy.

Financial Forecast

Companies in the financial sector use TensorFlow to predict market trends and manage risks. One example is the implementation of LSTM models for forecasting time series such as stock prices.

python

```
model = tf.keras.Sequential([
    tf.keras.layers.LSTM(64, return_sequences=True,
input_shape=(30, 5)),
    tf.keras.layers.LSTM(32),
    tf.keras.layers.Dense(1)
])

model.compile(optimizer='adam', loss='mse')
model.fit(train_data, train_labels, epochs=50, batch_size=32,
validation_data=(test_data, test_labels))
```

Automated Medical Diagnosis

In healthcare, TensorFlow is widely used for analyzing medical images such as X-rays and MRIs. Convolutional networks trained on large datasets provide accurate and fast diagnoses.

python

```
model = tf.keras.Sequential([
    tf.keras.layers.Conv2D(32, (3, 3), activation='relu',
input_shape=(256, 256, 1)),
    tf.keras.layers.MaxPooling2D((2, 2)),
    tf.keras.layers.Conv2D(64, (3, 3), activation='relu'),
    tf.keras.layers.MaxPooling2D((2, 2)),
    tf.keras.layers.Flatten(),
    tf.keras.layers.Dense(128, activation='relu'),
    tf.keras.layers.Dense(1, activation='sigmoid')
])

model.compile(optimizer='adam', loss='binary_crossentropy',
metrics=['accuracy'])
model.fit(train_images, train_labels, epochs=20, batch_size=64,
validation_data=(test_images, test_labels))
```

Large-scale applications with TensorFlow demonstrate its ability to address complex enterprise challenges. The combination of advanced tools, distributed training support and integration with cloud infrastructure allows companies to innovate and stand out in their markets. By exploring success stories and implementing effective strategies, organizations can leverage the power of TensorFlow to create scalable and impactful solutions.

CHAPTER 25: PRACTICAL PROJECTS FOR BEGINNERS AND ADVANCED

Learning becomes more effective when applied to practical projects. Working on real-world problems not only consolidates theoretical concepts, but also develops critical skills for dealing with challenges in diverse scenarios. This chapter presents project suggestions for beginners and advanced users, allowing readers of all levels to explore TensorFlow in a hands-on way. Each project is accompanied by challenges that encourage customization and real-world problem solving.

Practical Projects for Beginners

The beginner-friendly projects are designed to help you understand the fundamentals of TensorFlow, such as manipulating data, building models, and running inferences.

Project 1: Digit Recognition with MNIST

This project involves building a simple classifier for the famous MNIST dataset. It helps you understand how to configure, train, and evaluate a model.

Dataset Configuration

Load the MNIST dataset using TensorFlow and process the data for training.

python

```
import tensorflow as tf

# Loading the MNIST dataset
(X_train, y_train), (X_test, y_test) =
tf.keras.datasets.mnist.load_data()

# Normalizing the data
X_train = X_train / 255.0
X_test = X_test / 255.0

# Expanding dimensions for compatibility with CNNs
X_train = X_train[..., tf.newaxis]
X_test = X_test[..., tf.newaxis]
```

Model Construction

Create a convolutional neural network to classify digits.

python

```
model = tf.keras.Sequential([
    tf.keras.layers.Conv2D(32, (3, 3), activation='relu',
input_shape=(28, 28, 1)),
    tf.keras.layers.MaxPooling2D((2, 2)),
    tf.keras.layers.Flatten(),
    tf.keras.layers.Dense(128, activation='relu'),
    tf.keras.layers.Dense(10, activation='softmax')
])
```

Training and Assessment

Compile and train the model with the preprocessed dataset.

python

```
model.compile(optimizer='adam',
loss='sparse_categorical_crossentropy', metrics=['accuracy'])
model.fit(X_train, y_train, epochs=5, batch_size=32)
```

```
model.evaluate(X_test, y_test)
```

Challenges:

1. Add regularization techniques such as Dropout.
2. Experiment with different network architectures to improve accuracy.

Project 2: Sentiment Analysis with TensorFloIn

Build a sentiment analysis model to classify comments as positive or negative.

Dataset Configuration

Use a dataset of short texts and prepare it for the model.

python

```
from tensorflow.keras.preprocessing.text import Tokenizer
from tensorflow.keras.preprocessing.sequence import
pad_sequences

# Text data
texts = ["I love this product", "This is the worst experience ever",
"Amazing quality", "Not worth the price"]
labels = [1, 0, 1, 0]

# Tokenizing texts
tokenizer = Tokenizer(num_words=1000)
tokenizer.fit_on_texts(texts)
sequences = tokenizer.texts_to_sequences(texts)
X = pad_sequences(sequences, maxlen=10)
y = tf.convert_to_tensor(labels)
```

Model Construction

Develop an LSTM network to capture the sequential nature of texts.

python

```
model = tf.keras.Sequential([
    tf.keras.layers.Embedding(input_dim=1000,
output_dim=32, input_length=10),
    tf.keras.layers.LSTM(32, return_sequences=True),
    tf.keras.layers.LSTM(16),
    tf.keras.layers.Dense(1, activation='sigmoid')
])
```

Training

Compile and train the model with the texts and labels.

python

```
model.compile(optimizer='adam', loss='binary_crossentropy',
metrics=['accuracy'])
model.fit(X, y, epochs=10, batch_size=2)
```

Challenges:

1. Implement the analysis on a larger dataset, such as IMDb.
2. Adjust the architecture to improve accuracy for different types of text.

Advanced Projects

Advanced projects challenge readers to implement solutions to complex problems by leveraging TensorFlow's most advanced features.

Project 3: Medical Image Segmentation

This project uses convolutional networks to segment medical images such as x-rays.

Dataset Configuration

Use a dataset of segmented medical images.

python

```
import numpy as np

# Loading simulated data
X = np.random.rand(100, 128, 128, 1) # Input images
y = np.random.randint(0, 2, (100, 128, 128, 1)) # Segmented
masks
```

Model Construction

Implement a U-Net, a common architecture for segmentation.

python

```
inputs = tf.keras.layers.Input((128, 128, 1))
conv1 = tf.keras.layers.Conv2D(64, (3, 3), activation='relu',
padding='same')(inputs)
conv1 = tf.keras.layers.Conv2D(64, (3, 3), activation='relu',
padding='same')(conv1)
pool1 = tf.keras.layers.MaxPooling2D((2, 2))(conv1)

conv2 = tf.keras.layers.Conv2D(128, (3, 3), activation='relu',
padding='same')(pool1)
conv2 = tf.keras.layers.Conv2D(128, (3, 3), activation='relu',
padding='same')(conv2)
up1 = tf.keras.layers.Conv2DTranspose(64, (2, 2), strides=(2, 2),
padding='same')(conv2)
concat1 = tf.keras.layers.concatenate([up1, conv1])
```

```
outputs = tf.keras.layers.Conv2D(1, (1, 1), activation='sigmoid')
(concat1)
model = tf.keras.models.Model(inputs, outputs)
```

Training

Train the model with the dataset.

python

```
model.compile(optimizer='adam', loss='binary_crossentropy',
metrics=['accuracy'])
model.fit(X, y, epochs=20, batch_size=8)
```

Challenges:

1. Apply the model to real datasets, such as MICCAI Brain Tumor Segmentation.
2. Add techniques to improve segmentation, such as spatial attention.

Project 4: Recommendation System

Develop a recommendation system to suggest products or services based on user history.

Dataset Configuration

Prepare a dataset containing interactions between users and products.

python

```
user_ids = ["user1", "user2", "user3"]
item_ids = ["item1", "item2", "item3"]
ratings = [5, 3, 4]

dataset = tf.data.Dataset.from_tensor_slices((user_ids,
item_ids, ratings))
```

Model Construction

Implement a matrix factorization model.

python

```
class RecommenderModel(tf.keras.Model):
    def __init__(self, num_users, num_items, embedding_dim):
        super().__init__()
        self.user_embedding =
tf.keras.layers.Embedding(num_users, embedding_dim)
        self.item_embedding =
tf.keras.layers.Embedding(num_items, embedding_dim)

    def call(self, inputs):
        user_vector = self.user_embedding(inputs[0])
        item_vector = self.item_embedding(inputs[1])
        return tf.reduce_sum(user_vector * item_vector, axis=1)
```

Training

Train the model to predict interactions between users and items.

python

```
model = RecommenderModel(num_users=100, num_items=50,
embedding_dim=16)
model.compile(optimizer='adam', loss='mse')
model.fit(dataset.batch(16), epochs=10)
```

Challenges:

1. Use real data from a public dataset, like MovieLens.
2. Add additional features such as interaction time or item categories.

The hands-on projects presented in this chapter provide a solid foundation for applying TensorFlow to real-world problems. By addressing these challenges, you will be prepared to implement advanced, customized and highly effective solutions. Tweak, innovate, and explore the limits of deep learning with creativity and persistence.

FINAL CONCLUSION

We have reached the end of our journey through the world of TensorFlow, and it is time to reflect on the topics we explored, consolidate what we learned, and recognize the effort dedicated to mastering this powerful tool. This book was designed to be more than a technical guide — it is a gateway to transforming ideas into practical solutions, applicable in a variety of areas. Let's recap the main themes covered and highlight how each chapter contributed to building a solid and comprehensive foundation.

Chapter Summary

Chapter 1: Introduction to TensorFlow
We explore the history and evolution of TensorFlow, highlighting how it became one of the most used platforms in deep learning. We compare its functionalities with other libraries and discuss its impacts on the technological scenario.

Chapter 2: Environment Configuration
We guide the reader through installing TensorFlow on different operating systems and present tools such as Google Colab, essential for those who want to start deep learning projects without major technical barriers.

Chapter 3: Tensor Fundamentals

We discuss the structure of tensors, their fundamental properties and operations. This chapter laid the foundation for working with structured data and exploring the mathematical potential of TensorFlow.

Chapter 4: Data Structures in TensorFlow
We analyze the differences between NumPy tensors and arrays, showing how to integrate and manipulate datasets for deep learning projects.

Chapter 5: Introduction to Keras
We present the Keras API, highlighting its functionalities for building sequential and functional models. This chapter was crucial in familiarizing the reader with a simple and powerful interface.

Chapter 6: Model Training
We explore the complete model training cycle, from forward pass and backpropagation to hyperparameter configuration, illustrating how to optimize performance.

Chapter 7: Activation Functions
We discuss the main activation functions, such as ReLU, Sigmoid and Softmax, explaining their uses in different scenarios and the impacts on neural networks.

Chapter 8: Model Regularization
We show techniques such as Dropout and L2 regularization, which are essential for avoiding overfitting and improving model generalization.

Chapter 9: Datasets and Pipelines with tf.data
We determine how to create and manipulate efficient datasets with the API tf.data, ensuring optimized and scalable pipelines for data processing.

Chapter 10: Convolutional Networks (CNNs)
We explore the basis of CNNs and their application in computer vision, including the implementation of image classifiers.

Chapter 11: Recurrent Networks (RNNs)
We cover networks such as LSTMs and GRUs, essential for processing time series and sequences.

Chapter 12: Transfer Learning
We highlight the reuse of pre-trained models, saving time and resources when applying transferred learning to new problems.

Chapter 13: Generative Adversarial Networks (GANs)
We introduce the concept and implementation of GANs, an advanced technique for generating realistic data.

Chapter 14: Transformers
We look at Transformers, their innovative structure and impact on natural language processing, with BERT and GPT implementation examples.

Chapter 15: Visualization with TensorBoard
We demonstrate how to monitor training metrics, analyze gradients, and visualize model graphs using TensorBoard.

Chapter 16: Applications in IoT
We explore how TensorFlow Lite is used in embedded devices, enabling edge computing in IoT applications.

Chapter 17: Distributed Training
We analyze strategies for training models on clusters and multiple GPUs, accelerating large-scale learning processes.

Chapter 18: Model Export and Deployment
We detail how to export models to production and deploy them with TensorFlow Serving and cloud services.

Chapter 19: Optimizers and Loss Functions
We discuss the main optimizers and loss functions, showing how to choose the optimal options for each task.

Chapter 20: Benchmarking and Optimization
We teach you how to identify performance bottlenecks and implement practical optimizations for greater computational efficiency.

Chapter 21: Security and Robustness in Models
We address strategies to protect models against adversarial attacks and ensure robustness in critical scenarios.

Chapter 22: Case Studies
We present real examples of applications with TensorFlow, highlighting solutions in classification, NLP and computer vision.

Chapter 23: TensorFlow and the Future of AI

We discuss emerging trends in AI, including federated learning, quantum computing, and generative AI, highlighting TensorFlow's role in these advances.

Chapter 24: Large-Scale Applications
We demonstrate how to integrate TensorFlow into enterprise systems, exploring success stories in recommendation, financial forecasting and medical diagnosis.

Chapter 25: Practical Projects for Beginners and Advanced
We suggest projects to consolidate learning, encouraging the reader to apply TensorFlow to real challenges, from basic problems to complex solutions.

As I reach the end of this book, I want to express my sincerest gratitude. Each page is written with the aim of making your learning journey more accessible, structured and practical. The effort you've put into exploring each chapter is a reflection of your determination to master TensorFlow and apply that knowledge to turn ideas into reality.

Whether you're a beginner or a seasoned professional, your commitment to learning and constant pursuit of innovation are inspiring. It is through readers like you that the potential of artificial intelligence is realized, positively impacting our lives and shaping the future.

Yours sincerely,
Diego Rodrigues and Team!

www.ingramcontent.com/pod-product-compliance
Lightning Source LLC
LaVergne TN
LVHW051235050326
832903LV00028B/2413

9798311845892